THE
BRITISH MUSEUM
COOKBOOK

THE
BRITISH MUSEUM
COOKBOOK

————————

MICHELLE BERRIEDALE-JOHNSON

British Museum Publications

© 1987 MICHELLE BERRIEDALE-JOHNSON

PUBLISHED BY BRITISH MUSEUM PUBLICATIONS LIMITED
46 BLOOMSBURY STREET, LONDON WC1B 3QQ

THIRD IMPRESSION 1988

BRITISH LIBRARY CATALOGUING IN PUBLICATION DATA

BERRIEDALE-JOHNSON, MICHELLE
THE BRITISH MUSEUM COOKBOOK.
1. COOKERY, INTERNATIONAL
I. TITLE   II. BRITISH MUSEUM
641.5   TX725.A1

ISBN 0 · 7141 · 1663 · 7

DESIGNED AND ILLUSTRATED BY
MORRISON DALLEY DESIGN PARTNERSHIP
TYPESET IN GOUDY OLD STYLE AND BEMBO BY
ROWLAND PHOTOTYPESETTING LTD
PRINTED BY
ST EDMUNDSBURY PRESS LTD,
BURY ST EDMUNDS, SUFFOLK

CONTENTS

INTRODUCTION

To return home after a visit to the British Museum and to relive the experience by reading your guide book or admiring your postcards is wonderful, but how much better if you could also 'taste' your visit by recreating the dishes that the ancient civilisations, whose art works and artefacts are now displayed in glass cases, actually ate and enjoyed? Such was the inspiration behind this book.

The recreation of the foods of even so recent a period as eighteenth-century England does of course present problems. Some ingredients are no longer available, others have changed their nature so much as to be scarcely recognisable by our ancestors. Eighteenth-century recipe books are rather vague in their instructions; cooking equipment – ovens, hobs, utensils – have all changed dramatically. Tastes have also changed and what might have appealed to our great-great-great-grandparents might fill us with horror – and *vice versa*. But if recreating the dishes of our own country a mere two hundred years ago is difficult, how could one seriously hope to recreate the menus of people who lived four thousand years ago, in an entirely different part of the world?

The answer is of course that one cannot; or at least one cannot do it exactly. What we have tried to do instead is to recreate a flavour of what fashionable ancient Greek society in Athens, Anglo-Saxon peasants in their villages, early seventeenth-century Italians or late medieval Frenchmen might have eaten. Wherever possible – in other words wherever they exist – I have based the recipes in the book on original receipts, instructions or descriptions of dishes. Where this is not possible (there are, for example, no extant ancient Greek, Persian, Egyptian or Aztec recipes) I have used the foods which we know to have been available to these peoples, and the techniques which we know they had mastered, to create dishes which *could* have been eaten by them.

Fortunately, in many of the areas involved – the Mediterranean basin in particular – food preparation is extremely traditional so that many of the dishes which are prepared today have their roots way back in the mists of time. The melokhia soup prepared by a modern Egyptian housewife, for example, might as easily have been prepared by her ancestor whose husband was involved in the construction of the great pyramids.

The idea was to suggest at least one complete meal for each collection in the Museum, so that if your particular interest was in Imperial Rome, you could create for yourselves an 'Imperial Roman' dinner. To this end we have included a suggested 'Menu' in the introduction to each section. There is of course no necessity to use the dishes only in this context as many of them are excellent and would fit well into any ordinary twentieth-century meal.

Although I have been to great pains to recreate the flavour of the original food, I have also taken some account of modern tastes and sensibilities. If the original would have been unpalatably strong, salty, sweet or rich, I have tempered it to what appeared to me to be an acceptable flavour. Even so, many of the tastes will be unusual and the food combinations in some of the recipes may come as something of a cultural shock. Please do not be put off by what looks like a weird mixture. Years of working with old recipes has taught me to have far more faith in them than I do in the average twentieth-century one. They may look bizarre but, in the vast majority of cases, they work.

Because we are covering such a wide canvas of foods, raw materials for some of the recipes in the book were obviously going to cause a problem. However, I have tried to restrict ingredients to things which are obtainable in most urban areas in Europe and North America, even if it does require a little searching. I have suggested sources of supply in the introduction to each recipe.

Similarly, I have only suggested using equipment which is available to most domestic cooks. One of the advantages of working with old recipes is that our forefathers had far less in the way of equipment than we do, so we tend to have an easier life of it. How much less effort for example, to purée a mixture in a food processor – or to buy ready ground almonds – than to have to spend hours pounding away with a pestle and mortar. How much simpler to set a timer for fifteen minutes than to have to say ten 'Our Fathers' – which was how the medieval cooks timed their dishes; in those days everyone knew their prayers whereas no one could have read a clock even if they had one!

There is no way that any cook or culinary historian could pretend to a knowledge of even a tithe of the cuisines and their histories which we have covered in the book. I am therefore immensely grateful to my colleagues in the cookery world who have charted the territory so excellently and who have, either in person or by their writings, so generously allowed me an insight into their own culinary traditions.

High amongst these I must rank Claudia Roden who is a mine of information on the foods of the Middle East and especially of her native Egypt, and whose recipes I have quoted on pp. 13, 16, 18, 43, 47. Her *New Book of Middle Eastern Food*, along with those of Tess Mallos (*The Complete Middle East Cookbook*), Suzy Benghiat (*Middle Eastern Cookery*) and Robin Howe (*Greek Cooking*) were my constant companions for some months. In the context of ancient Greek cooking, I am also most grateful to Christopher Driver who introduced me to, and gave me access to his copy of, all twenty-five volumes of Athenaeus' *Deipnosophistae*, our main source of information about the eating habits of classical Greece.

The chapter on Pre-Conquest America would not have existed without the generous help of Elisabeth Lambert Ortiz, whose researches into the eating habits of the Incas, Aztecs and Mayans have continued over many years and whose books on Latin American food are fascinating. Again, I am most grateful to her for allowing me to quote her recipes on pp. 75, 76, 78, 83.

The same must be said for the food of China, which I dearly love to eat, but about whose history and cookery methods I am, or was, woefully ignorant. Kenneth Lo, whose interest in the culinary history of his country should have a wider airing than these pages, instructed me, advised me and generously allowed me to use and adapt his recipes on pp. 144–51.

I have also to thank Anne del Conte for the most enjoyable week during which I picked her brains and combed her well-stocked library in pursuit of Renaissance Italian delicacies; and for allowing me to use her own realisations of them on pp. 106, 110, 114.

As for the food of ancient, medieval and modern England and northern Europe, I fear I am entirely responsible for the recipes which follow, although I am most grateful to John Clark of the Museum of London for his advice on the availability of Anglo-Saxon foodstuffs and cooking implements. However, my most heartfelt thanks must go to all those cooks, gastronomes and *bon viveurs* from Richard II to Mrs Beeton who have cared enough about what they ate to experiment with it, pay huge sums for rare ingredients – and rare cooks to work with them – devote hours to mixing and stirring, testing and tasting, and finally to take the time to write it all down, thus creating so rich a culinary literature for us to delve in. At the end of the book I include some details of the cooks and culinary writers mentioned.

An asterisk ★ by a recipe means that it was based on or taken from the work of one of the people acknowledged above.

My last, but absolutely not least, thanks must go to British Museum Publications for thinking of and then asking me to write the book; to its editor, Emma Myers with whom it has been such a pleasure to work, and especially to Morrison Dalley whose designs have so evocatively created the atmosphere of each collection.

MBJ 1986

ANCIENT PERSIA

The kingdoms of Persia, Assyria and Babylon with their fabulous wealth, shady palaces, tinkling fountains, beautiful women and exotic feasts have long been recognised as the pinnacle of ancient civilisation. Gastronomically, their situation at the heart of the 'fertile crescent' provided them with wonderful fresh fruits and vegetables while their nearness to India gave them access to the spices and the rich culinary tradition of the east.

Persian cookery has always been famed for the delicacy of its sauces subtly combining sour pomegranate juice or verjuice made from unripe grapes, with the sweetness of fresh fruits and spices. It is these flavours, along with a passion for fresh herbs and the exquisite cooking of the rice which accompanies every meal, which have had most influence on the cooking of its neighbours.

Meats and fish are served roast or baked but Persian cooks prefer to stew them long and slowly with vegetables, herbs, spices and fruits in Khoreshtha or sauces which more nearly resemble a western stew. A dish of chilau rice with a khoresh forms the centrepiece of almost every meal accompanied by bowls of fresh herbs, salads, 'kukus' or egg cakes flavoured with herbs, flat Persian bread, nuts and fresh fruits. The fruits are seldom dressed as they are rightly thought too good to be capable of improvement. While wine and spirits were common in ancient Persia, in modern Iran tea and yoghourt, mixed with water and often flavoured with herbs, are drunk with all meals.

To serve a Persian lunch or dinner you should first acquire a Persian rug . . . Lay it on the ground protected by a plastic or leather sheet and covered with a cloth, then arrange cushions around it for your guests. Food is now seldom eaten in the traditional manner with the fingers of the right hand, but off china plates with spoons and forks.

Include at least one khoresh with rice, a kuku or soup as a first course or appetiser, bowls of fresh herbs and radishes, cucumbers, and cos or romaine lettuce in a salad. Yoghourt, oil and vinegar should be available to dress it. Really ripe fresh fruits and

MENU

A KUKUYE SABSI

OR

YOGHOURT SOUP WITH WALNUTS

CHILAU RICE WITH A KHORESH
FAISINJAN

OR

KHORESH WITH SPINACH & PRUNES

SALAD OF LETTUCE WITH
CUCUMBER & RADISHES

BOWLS OF FRESH HERBS

FLAT PERSIAN BREAD
PITTA BREAD

FRESH FRUITS & NUTS

A MACERATED FRUIT SALAD

OR

APPLE & PEAR SHERBET

BLACK TEA OR ABDUG OR PERSIAN
YOGHOURT DRINK

nuts will suffice as dessert unless you want to indulge in a sherbet or a dish of chilled, macerated fruit on a hot evening.

NB A bowl filled with sprigs of parsley, chives, mint, dill, cress, coriander, tarragon or any herb which happens to be available will normally be found on the table at a Persian meal. According to an ancient belief, women who eat the herbs at the end of the meal with bread and cheese will have no difficulty in keeping their husbands.

ESHKENEH SHIRAZI★
or PERSIAN YOGHOURT SOUP
SERVES SIX

Yoghourt has been used for many centuries in Persia, especially in the making of soups where it is both cooked as an integral part of the soup and added at the end. The Eshkeneh Shirazi is the most delicious speciality of the city of Shiraz, fresh flavoured and light enough for a hot summer's evening.

2 tablespoons butter

1–2 onions, finely chopped

2 tablespoons plain flour

50 g • 2 oz coarsely chopped walnuts or pecans

a bunch of fenugreek, finely chopped *or*

1 teaspoon fenugreek seeds

1 litre • 1¾ pints • 4¼ cups hot water

salt and black pepper

600 ml • 1 pint • 2½ cups

plain yoghourt, live if possible

Melt the butter in a large pan and fry the onions till they are a pale golden colour. Add the flour and stir over a very low heat for a few minutes until they are well blended. Add the nuts and the fenugreek, pour in a ladleful of hot water and beat vigorously, then slowly add the rest of the water, stirring constantly. Season with salt and pepper. Bring to the boil and simmer, covered for 15–20 minutes till the soup has thickened slightly and lost its floury taste. Beat the yoghourt vigorously, add a ladleful of the hot soup and beat well. Gradually pour the mixture back into the soup, stirring all the while, then reheat very gently to just below boiling point. Adjust the seasoning to taste and serve at once.

KUKUYE SABSI
or HERB & SPINACH 'EGGAH'
or OMELETTE
SERVES SIX

Of ancient origin, the Persian 'kukus' (called 'eggah's elsewhere in the Middle East) are closer to Spanish tortillas than French omelettes. Like egg cakes in texture, they are bursting with rich fillings, baked in the oven, or long and slowly on a hob, and are as good eaten cold as hot. You can change the herbs (and their quantities) according to personal preference and availability, but do try to use fresh ones if at all possible.

2 tablespoons olive *or* sunflower oil
2 leeks, cleaned and chopped finely
350 g • 12 oz fresh, washed and chopped spinach
or 150 g • 6 oz frozen leaf spinach,
defrosted and well drained
12 eggs
8 spring onions *or* scallions chopped finely
2 handfuls of parsley, chopped finely
1–2 handfuls fresh coriander, chopped finely *or*
1 teaspoon of dried
2 sprigs of fresh tarragon, chopped *or*
½ teaspoon of dried
handful of fresh chives, chopped
1 small sprig of dill, chopped *or*
¼ teaspoon dried
2–4 sprigs of fresh mint, chopped *or*
1 teaspoon dried
40 g • 1½ oz chopped walnuts *or* pecans
40 g • 1½ oz pine nuts
salt and pepper

Heat the oil in a large, flat, pan and gently cook the leeks till they are just softened. If the spinach is fresh, add it to the pan and wilt it for a couple of minutes. Beat the eggs in a bowl with a fork, then add the leek and spinach, the herbs and the nuts and season well. Pour the mixture back into the pan, cover and cook the kuku over a very gentle heat for approximately 25 minutes or till it is well set. Uncover it and brown the top under a grill.

Alternatively, the kuku can be cooked in a well buttered dish in a moderate oven (180°C • 350°F • Gas Mark 4), covered for the first 20 minutes, then uncovered to allow the top to brown. The kuku can be served in wedges, warm or cold, as a starter or cut into bite sized pieces and served with drinks.

CHILAU RICE
SERVES SIX

Persia has always been famous for the delicacy of its rice and the wonderful sauces that are served with it. There are an infinite variety of them – incorporating meat, poultry, fish, vegetables, beans, fruits, both dried and fresh, herbs and spices – but always served with rice. The sweet and sour combinations of flavours, refined over the centuries, are delicate and delicious so it is worth trying to unearth the right ingredients. Chilau rice certainly repays the small extra effort in preparing it.

350 g • 12 oz Basmati rice – rinsed or soaked for
1–3 hours in lukewarm water
(opinions differ but soaking seems to give a
slightly lighter texture)
salt
approximately 75 g • 3 oz butter

Fill a large pan with plenty of boiling water and salt generously. Sprinkle in the rinsed or soaked rice, bring back to the boil and cook briskly for 4–8 minutes or till the rice is almost but not quite cooked. Drain and rinse again under hot water. Put half the butter in the bottom of a pan, allow it to melt then put in the rice and stir. Put the remaining butter over the top, cover the pan with a cloth to absorb the steam, and a tight fitting lid and cook over a very low heat for 30–40 minutes. The rice on the bottom should form a crisp golden crust, called 'dig', which is delicious and is served separately – normally to the guest of honour. The rest of the rice is served with assorted khoreshtha (see over).

LAMB & SPINACH KHORESH★
SERVES SIX

Lamb is the favourite Persian meat but there is no reason why you should not substitute beef or chicken in this khoresh. Similarly, feel free to alter the quantities or types of spices.

3 large onions, chopped

4 tablespoons olive *or* sunflower oil

750 g • 1½ lb stewing lamb, well trimmed and dried on kitchen paper towel

100 g • 4 oz plump, pitted prunes

1 medium cooking apple, peeled and diced

2 teaspoons *each* ground cinnamon, nutmeg and ginger

handful of chopped fresh coriander *or* 1 teaspoon of dried

salt and pepper

1.2 litres • 2 pints • 5 cups water

225 g • 8 oz fresh spinach, washed and roughly chopped, *or* 100 g • 4 oz frozen leaf spinach

Gently fry the onions in the oil till they are beginning to soften, increase the heat, add the lamb pieces and fry briskly till the meat is well browned all over. Remove from the heat and add the prunes, apples, spices, herbs and seasoning, stir them well together then gradually add the water. Bring the khoresh to the boil and simmer it very gently for 1½–2 hours or till the meat is almost cooked – you can successfully use a slow cooker for this. Add the spinach and continue to cook for a further 30–45 minutes till the meat is really tender and the flavours well amalgamated. Adjust the seasoning to taste and serve with chilau rice.

KHORESH FAISINJAN★
SERVES FOUR

This is a wonderfully rich khoresh designed for wild duck or pheasant, but which tastes just as good with chicken or farmhouse duck. You should be able to get the pomegranate juice in a Middle Eastern or Greek delicatessen.

1 *or* 2 duck (depending on size), 2 pheasants *or* a chicken – jointed

2 tablespoons olive *or* vegetable oil

1 large onion

225 g • 8 oz coarsely chopped walnuts or pecans

5 cm • 2 inch cinnamon stick

1 tablespoon brown sugar

salt and pepper

350 ml • 12 fl oz • 1½ cups pomegranate juice

juice of ½–1 lemon

Heat the oil in an ovenproof casserole and brown the jointed bird thoroughly on both sides. Remove from the pan and set aside. Brown the onion in the same oil then return the bird to the

pan. Add the nuts, cinnamon, sugar, seasoning and the juice. Cover the casserole and cook in a moderate oven (180°C • 350°F • Gas Mark 4) for 1½–2½ hours or till the meat is really tender and falling off the bone. Carefully remove the bird from the casserole, put it on a dish and return to the oven to crisp up the skin slightly. Meanwhile, skim the excess fat from the sauce (if you are using a duck there will be a great deal) and save it

for other uses. Adjust the seasoning of the sauce to taste, adding as much lemon juice as you find necessary to set off the sweet richness of the sauce. Serve the bird with chilau rice with the sauce spooned over it.

KHOCHAF *or* KHOSHAF *or* DRIED FRUIT SALAD
SERVES SIX

Fruit salads made from dried rather than fresh fruits and macerated rather than cooked are traditional favourites, especially in ancient Persia (modern Iran). The combination of fruits can be altered to suit your own taste although purists insist that apricots and raisins alone are allowed. Pomegranate seeds can be used for colour and the nuts added at the beginning or at the end; I prefer the latter as that way they retain a slight crunch.

225 g • 8 oz dried apricots
100 g • 4 oz plump raisins
1 teaspoon pomegranate seeds *optional*
approximately 50 g • 2 oz sugar
1 tablespoon *each* rose and orange blossom water
25 g • 1 oz pistachio nuts or toasted pine nuts, *or*
15 g • ½ oz of each

Put the apricots and raisins in a bowl with the pomegranate seeds and the sugar; the amount of sugar you use is a matter of personal taste. Cover with water, sprinkle with the rose and orange blossom water; cover and leave the fruits to soak in a cool place for at least 48 hours. The syrup will acquire a delicious flavour and a deep, rich colour from the fruits. Mix in the nuts and serve lightly chilled, alone or with lightly whipped cream.

PRUNES STUFFED WITH WALNUTS★
SERVES SIX

For prune addicts this 'dessert of ancient origin' is irresistible.

24 plump, pitted prunes (if you cannot get pitted prunes you merely have to remove the stones, keeping the prunes as complete as possible)
24 large walnut halves
150 ml • 5 fl oz *each* water and red wine
200 ml • 7 fl oz double *or* heavy cream
approximately 2 tablespoons sugar
1 tablespoon rose water

Stuff the prunes with the walnut halves, squashing them well together to keep the nuts in place. Put the prunes in a pan with the water and wine, bring slowly to the boil and simmer gently for approximately 30 minutes. Pour into a glass bowl or individual glasses and cool. Whisk the cream till it just holds its shape, then add sugar to taste and the rosewater. Spoon the cream over the prunes and chill well before serving. The prunes are even better if left for 24 hours before being served.

APPLE & PEAR SHERBET
SERVES SIX

Sherbets are an unusual way of serving fresh fruits – deliciously cool and refreshing in the steaming heat of a Persian summer.

1 lemon

2 large, tart eating apples

2 large, ripe pears

2 tablespoons icing *or* confectioner's sugar

2 tablespoons rose water

6 large ice cubes, crushed *or* 1 large glassful of

crushed ice

Peel the rind off the lemon as thinly as possible and cut it into slivers; squeeze the juice from the fruit. Peel and core the apples and pears and grate them into a bowl. Sprinkle on the lemon juice to prevent them discolouring, then stir in the sugar and rose water. Cover the bowl and chill the mixture for several hours. Approximately half an hour before you want to serve the dessert, put the fruit with its juices and the ice cubes or crushed ice into a food processor or liquidiser and blend briefly to reduce the mixture to a coarse pulp. Pour it into six glasses or a glass bowl and return it to the freezer for 15–30 minutes (although this may be risky if you're using the best crystal!); the mixture should be almost frozen but not quite. Serve sprinkled with the slivers of lemon rind.

CLASSICAL GREECE

Classical Greece was a land of trade; olive oil and wine in return for the more basic food stuffs which had been driven off the land by the desire to grow more (and therefore export more) olive oil and wine. The wine, particularly the vintages of Lesbos and Chios, were famous and probably quite sweet. They were fermented in vats heavily smeared with resin, hence the characteristic tang of Greek wine, and, in classical times, were drunk heavily diluted with water.

The heroes of antiquity had simple tastes which did not venture far beyond large and succulent roasts of goat, sheep or pig meat accompanied by plenty of bread. This diet was supplemented by barley gruels or porridges (the staple diet of the peasant), some green and root vegetables, goat's milk and goat's cheese, olives and, according to Alexis of Thurii in the fourth century BC, 'that god-given inheritance of our mother country, darling of my heart, a dried fig'. Since most of Greece is close to the sea, fish was abundant: tunny, mullet, mackerel, snapper, octopus, squid, sea urchins and all varieties of shell fish, grilled or baked in broth.

As the cities became more sophisticated, so did the food. Fourth-century BC Athens saw an explosion of culinary literature, none of which has alas survived except through the writings of Atheneaus, an amazingly garrulous second-century AD Egyptian whose twenty-five volumes of the *Deipno-sophistae* contains a plethora of information about the eating – and all other – habits of ancient Greece. According to Atheneaus, feasts became lavish, palates more refined, and professional gourmets such as Archestratus started to pronounce on the comparable virtues of fresh tunny from Byzantium and dried or salted tunny from the Black Sea. Song birds and poultry were now regularly served, cakes and sweetmeats rich in honey, nuts and seeds ended every feast and by the third century BC, the mezze or *hors d'oeuvre* table had arrived much to the horror of those who believed that a meal consisted of a decent roast with a loaf of bread.

In many ways, modern Greek cookery remains close to its roots – the fondness for spit-roast lamb and kid, radishes, lettuce and herbs such as mint and marjoram; the widespread use of goat and sheep's milk and olive oil, the passion

MENU

MEZZE TABLE

BRAISED TUNA FISH

ROAST LAMB OR KID

BRAISED LETTUCE OR CABBAGE

PITTA BREAD

HONEY CHEESECAKE

FIGS WITH ALMONDS
OR
HONEY & SESAME BALLS

for honey-rich sweetmeats. But modern 'made' dishes owe much to the arrival, after the Spanish conquest of South America, of the fruits of the *Solanaceae* family: peppers, aubergines or eggplants, tomatoes and potatoes. In an attempt to retain the flavour of classical Greece I have deliberately excluded all such dishes from the recipes which follow.

An authentic classical Greek meal should include a whole roast lamb or kid but if you do not want to run to those lengths, a good roast leg of lamb will make an acceptable substitute. Any modern Greek wine would be acceptable but, if you do wish to be authentic, look for a sweet one and dilute it with water.

MEZZE

The mezze table, now so typical a part of any Greek meal, first became popular in third-century BC Athenian 'society', though it was thoroughly disapproved of by the less fashion conscious who felt you could not get a decent meal out of 'all those dainty little dishes'.

A classical 'mezze table' could include an astonishing range of snacks: roast thrushes or nightingales, truffles, edible iris bulbs, mushrooms, olives in brine, radishes, pickled and smoked fishes, all kinds of shell fish, sea urchins, capers, pigs brains, marinated turnips, snails, artichokes, lettuce leaves, smoked and melted cheeses, and chick peas as well as the even more unlikely grasshoppers, crickets and peacock eggs.

As with a western *hors d'oeuvre*, a mezze table can include anything you fancy but if you want to give it a classical flavour make sure you serve at least some of the following, many of which can easily be bought in a good delicatessen:

hummus – a paste made from pounded chickpeas

large olives

large radishes

crisp lettuce leaves, preferably Cos lettuce

button mushrooms, raw *or* lightly cooked in olive oil with marjoram

artichoke hearts, cooked and marinated in oil and lemon juice

cockles, mussels *or* oysters stewed in olive oil

pickled fish (the recipe for Sogliole on p. 106 would be good)

taramasalata – dried and pressed mullet roe although smoked cod's roe is frequently and successfully substituted

feta *or* other hard goat's cheese

LENTIL SOUP
SERVES SIX–EIGHT

Lentil soup was the food of the poor in classical Greece, spurned, unwisely, by the intellectuals and gastronomes of Athens. This recipe makes a very thick soup, ideal for a cold winter's night; if you want it to be a little less filling, thin it with more water or stock and readjust the seasoning before serving it.

450 g • 1 lb red lentils, rinsed
3 medium onions, finely chopped
3 large cloves garlic, finely chopped
1 carrot, scrubbed and very finely chopped
1 stick celery, very finely chopped
120 ml • 4 fl oz • ½ cup olive oil
2 bay leaves and a generous pinch of marjoram
1.5 litres • 2½ pints • 6¼ cups water
60 ml • 2 fl oz • ¼ cup wine vinegar
salt and pepper

Put all the ingredients except the seasoning and vinegar in a large pan, bring slowly to the boil and simmer for 1 hour, stirring now and then to make sure that nothing sticks to the bottom. Remove the bay leaves and add the vinegar and seasoning. If you find it too thick, thin the soup with more water or a little stock and readjust the seasoning before serving.

GRILLED MULLET
SERVES SIX

Both red and grey mullets have been caught, grilled, baked, boiled and eaten all around the Mediterranean since time immemorial. It is the dried, salted, pressed roe of the grey mullet which should be used to make taramasalata although smoked cod's roe is often substituted, and it is the dried and salted roes which make the *avgotarho* or *batarekh* which are so popular all over the Middle East. But best of all, I think, is a really fresh fish, simply grilled.

6 small or 3 large red mullet, cleaned and scaled
2 handfuls of fresh herbs, finely chopped – any
of the following can be included but try to use
fresh rather than dried if possible; if not

substitute 1 mixed tablespoonful of the
same herbs, dried – thyme, rosemary, mint,
coriander, marjoram, chervil, parsley
3 tablespoons olive oil
juice of 1 lemon
salt and pepper

Mix the herbs, oil, lemon juice, salt and pepper well together and paint the inside and outside of the fish generously. Lay them on a griddle or under a grill (on aluminium foil so that you do not lose the juices into the bottom of the pan) and cook them for 4–10 minutes on each side, depending on the size of the fish, basting them every few minutes with the extra juices and what runs off the fish. Turn the fish over, paint the other side with the remaining juices and continue to cook till the fish is flaking from the bone. Serve at once, with any remaining juices, crusty fresh bread and a good green salad.

BRAISED TUNA FISH
SERVES SIX

Like mullet, tuna fish is a long time resident of the Mediterranean, frequently mentioned by Athenaeus and still to be found gracing the tables of Greek and Italian restaurants. It is however an immensely dense and dry fish so needs to be cooked with plenty of liquid. Fresh tuna is not always easy to get in northern climes but, if it is not available, tinned tuna is quite acceptable.

8 tablespoons olive oil (if you are using tinned tuna include the oil from the tin)

8 leeks, finely sliced

8 sticks celery, finely chopped

4 sprigs *each* of fresh rosemary and fresh thyme; if fresh is not available, 1 heaped teaspoon each of dried

salt and pepper

½ a medium cucumber, thinly sliced

300 ml • 10 fl oz • 2½ cups *each* water and dry white wine, Greek if at all possible

6 tuna steaks or 4 × 200 g • 7 oz tins tuna fish

Heat the oil in a large pan and gently cook the leeks and celery till they start to soften. Add the herbs, seasoning, cucumber, wine and water and mix well, then lay the tuna steaks on top of the vegetables. Cover the pan and simmer gently for 30–45 minutes, depending on the thickness of the steaks. Adjust the seasoning to taste and serve with plenty of rice and a good green salad. If you are using tinned tuna, break up the fish in large chunks into the vegetables and simmer for 15 minutes to heat the fish and amalgamate the flavours.

SPIT-ROAST LAMB, KID *or* SUCKING PIG

The heroes of ancient Greece were more concerned with battles than with baking, so, as long as the meat was tender and plentiful, accompanied by quantities of bread and washed down with copious drafts of wine, everyone was happy. Although modern Greek cooking includes many excellent 'made' dishes, the festive meal is still always a roast of lamb, kid or sucking pig – little different from the feast offered to Odysseus by the 'godlike Achilles' in Homeric times.

Whole lambs, kids or piglets are seldom available to the ordinary housewife, even if she felt capable of tackling them. But the slow roasting which produces such deliciously succulent meat works just as well on a small joint of lamb in an oven.

Should you find yourself with a whole animal and the facilities to roast it out of doors, it must be thoroughly cleaned, and well rubbed with salt and lemon juice both inside and out. In the case of lamb, the stomach opening must be tightly sewn up. The animal should then be securely attached to the spit. Lamb should be started at some distance from the fire to prevent scorching and gradually brought closer to the flame. The cooking should take around three hours and the meat should be constantly turned and basted with its own drippings mixed with butter, thyme and lemon juice. A piglet needs roughly the same treatment although the cooking time may be up to 4 hours.

However, judging the right distance of fire from meat to cook all parts of the animal without drying out the less fleshy parts is a matter of some skill and experience, so be warned. Both meats are best pulled apart in the fingers and eaten with salt, fresh bread and plenty of good rough wine.

To achieve the more plebeian end of a well roasted leg or shoulder of lamb you will need:

1 leg of lamb
4–6 cloves garlic, depending on size
juice of 1 lemon
2–3 tablespoons olive oil
1 teaspoon dried thyme or 2 teaspoons fresh, chopped
salt and pepper

Cut deep slits in the lamb and insert the garlic cloves. Mix the lemon juice, oil, thyme and seasoning well together then rub them thoroughly all over the lamb. Put the lamb in a roasting tin, raised on a rack if possible. Add 2 tablespoons of water to the basting mixture and pour it into the bottom of the roasting tin. Cook the meat for 20 minutes to the pound (for a pink middle), basting the joint with the juices every 10–15 minutes.

SAUSAGES
SERVES SIX

Animals, in classical Greece, were far too valuable for the smallest edible bit to be wasted. So, headmeat, entrails, intestines and all the other nourishing but less appealing parts of the sheep, goat or pig were chopped up, mixed with herbs and spices and made into sausages. If you do not wish to be quite so authentic, stewing lamb or pork makes an excellent substitute.

450 g • 1 lb untrimmed stewing lamb *or* pork, diced. You could also use cooked meat to make the sausages.

2 medium onions, roughly chopped

3 large cloves garlic

75 g • 3 oz brown breadcrumbs

approximately 20 fresh, chopped mint leaves *or*

2 teaspoons dried mint

2 teaspoons fresh chopped marjoram *or*

1 teaspoon of dried

1 teaspoon ground cumin

salt and pepper

180 ml • 6 fl oz • ¾ cup rough red wine

2 eggs

a little flour and olive oil

Put the meat through a mincer or mince it in a food processor along with the onion and garlic, breadcrumbs, herbs and spices, wine and eggs. Make sure the mixture is well amalgamated and season it generously. Roll it into sausage shapes or into flat cakes and coat lightly in flour. If you want to fry the sausages, heat the oil in a pan and fry them gently on all sides taking care that they do not stick to the bottom of the pan. If you prefer to grill or broil them, brush them with the olive oil before putting them on a rack under the grill or broiler. The sausages are as good cold as hot.

CHICKPEAS
SERVES SIX

In classical Greece fresh chickpeas, along with beans and other pulses, were used as a dessert while the dried variety were soaked, cooked and sometimes roasted so they could be eaten as a snack. Cooked as below they can be used either as a vegetable or as a salad. Like all pulses, they improve with keeping so should be made a couple of days before they are needed.

225 g • 8 oz dried chickpeas
1–2 medium onions, very finely chopped
4 cloves garlic, very finely chopped
large handful of fresh mint, parsley or coriander
or any combination of the three
4 tablespoons olive oil
salt and pepper to taste

Soak the chickpeas in plenty of water for a minimum of 8 hours. Dry them and rub them vigorously between your hands, then return them to a bowl of water and the skins will float to the top. Remove the skins and put the chickpeas in a large pan, generously covered in fresh water. Bring them to the boil and simmer gently for 3–4 hours or till they are soft; some people like to retain a slight crunch, others prefer them totally soft. Drain the peas and return them to the pan with the rest of the ingredients. Mix well and leave them over a *very* low heat for a further half hour. The chickpeas can be eaten at once but would be better left for 24 hours or more for the flavours to mature. They can then be eaten at room temperature or gently reheated.

CABBAGE WITH SPINACH & MINT *or* CORIANDER
SERVES SIX

A gruel of cabbage 'greens', turnips and barley formed the basis of the Greek peasant diet for many centuries but in the eyes of the more sophisticated city dwellers, cabbage had a far greater virtue: it was both an antidote to drunkenness and a hangover cure. According to Atheneaus the

Egyptians, who were great wine drinkers, always served boiled cabbage first on their bill of fare, while Theophrastus believed its effect to be so powerful that 'even the growing vine loathes the smell of cabbage'.

4 tablespoons olive oil

1 large onion, finely chopped

4 cloves garlic, finely chopped

450 g • 1 lb young green cabbage, chopped fairly finely

225 g • 8 oz spinach, well washed, dried and roughly chopped

2 medium courgettes *or zucchini*, wiped and sliced thickly

a generous handful of fresh mint *or* coriander, roughly chopped *or* 2 heaped teaspoons of dried

salt and pepper

Heat the oil in a large pan and gently cook the onion and garlic till it begins to soften. Add the cabbage and cook for a few minutes. Then add the spinach, courgettes and herbs, cover the pan and cook it over a very low heat for 15 minutes, stirring now and then to make sure the ingredients are well mixed. The vegetables should be cooked but still retain a little crunch in their stalks. Season to taste with salt and pepper and serve at once.

BRAISED LETTUCE
SERVES SIX

Lettuce was believed by the ancient Greeks to be a very efficient soporific – the corollary being that it was to be avoided by those amorously inclined. Nicander of Colophon, as quoted by Atheneaus, declares that: 'If a man not yet sixty should eat lettuce when he desires commerce with a woman, he might twist and turn the whole

night long without once accomplishing his desires, wringing his hands against stern fate instead of acting like man . . .' None the less, lettuce was highly esteemed, both raw and cooked. A muscular and flavoursome lettuce, such as a Cos, is the best if it is to be cooked.

4 tablespoons olive oil

2 medium onions, finely chopped

2 cloves garlic, very finely chopped

2 large Cos lettuces, washed, well dried and roughly chopped

12 sage leaves, chopped roughly *or* 1 teaspoon dried sage

120 ml • 4 fl oz • ½ cup white wine

salt and pepper

Heat the oil in a large pan and gently cook the onions and garlic till they begin to soften. Add the lettuce, sage and wine, cover the pan and continue to cook on a low heat for 5 minutes, stirring now and then to 'circulate' the lettuce. After 5 minutes the leaves should be wilted leaving the stems crisp. Season to taste with salt and pepper and serve at once.

HONEY CHEESECAKE

SERVES SIX

Archestratus, father of all gastronomes, is high in his praise of Athenian cheesecake. Indeed, he counsels all serious gourmets to reject 'common desserts such as boiled chick peas, beans, apples and dried figs as a sign of dire poverty. But to accept a cheesecake made in Athens; or failing that, if you can get one from somewhere else, go out and demand some Attic honey as that will make your cheesecake superb.' We cannot hope to rival the achievements of ancient Athens, but the modern version is very palatable. The cheesecake can be cooked on its own in a flan dish, like baked custard, or in a pastry case.

450 g • 1 lb *myzithra* (Greek cottage cheese),
cottage or curd cheese
3 tablespoons honey
juice 2 lemons
4 eggs
1 tablespoon orange flower water
1 teaspoon ground cinnamon *or* 12 finely
chopped fresh mint leaves *optional*

23 cm • 9 inch shortcrust pastry flan case, baked
blind *optional*

Put the cheese with the honey, lemon juice, eggs and orange flower water in a processor and process till completely mixed. Add the cinnamon or mint, if you wish to use them, and mix thoroughly. Spoon the mixture into a flan or soufflé dish or into the pre-prepared pastry case. Bake in a moderately cool oven (160°C • 325°F • Gas Mark 3) for 30 minutes or till the cheesecake is slightly risen and lightly tanned. Serve warm.

HONEY & BARLEY PUDDING
SERVES SIX

A barley gruel or porridge was the staple diet of the ancient Greek peasant, enlivened with a little honey, some goat's milk or ewe's milk cheese, bulked out with bread and washed down with water, goat's milk or, on a good day, wine. And it still makes an excellent pudding, if a little reminiscent of the nursery – which, to many people, would be all in its favour.

100 g • 4 oz pot barley
approximately 600 ml • 1 pint • 2½ cups goat's or ewe's milk, if available, if not, cow's milk
honey
plain, live yoghourt – goat, ewe *or* cow
toasted sesame seeds or toasted pine nuts

Put the barley in a pan generously covered with the milk and allow to soak for 10 minutes. Bring gradually to the boil and simmer very gently for approximately 2 hours or till the barley is totally soft. Add extra milk if the barley looks as though it is getting dry. Remove it from the heat and allow it to cool completely; the remaining liquid will become almost totally jellied. You can set it aside at this point as it will keep in the fridge for up to a week. Serve the barley warm or at room temperature with a generous helping of honey and yoghourt on each portion and liberally sprinkled with sesame seeds or pine nuts, or both.

DRIED FIGS WITH CHOPPED ALMONDS

Cut as many fresh figs as you want to use in half and flatten them as much as possible. Dry them in the sun, if it is available, or in a very low oven, till the outside is quite dry but the inside still sticky.

Sprinkle one half of each fig with toasted chopped almonds and press the two halves of the figs together. You can also make this sweetmeat with pre-dried figs as long as you make sure that they are really plump and soft. Split them in half and press the almonds on as above. You may want to cut them in halves or quarters to serve.

HONEY & SESAME BALLS
MAKES TWENTY TO TWENTY-FIVE BALLS

In classical, as in modern Greece immensely rich and sweet, honey-filled 'sweetmeats' are nibbled as snacks with chilled water, spiced wines or coffee between or after meals. Sometimes they are merely dried fruits, such as the much loved fig (see p. 33). Other sweetmeats are combinations of honey and nuts or seeds which, in modern Greece, are usually wrapped in paper thin filo paste. In all cases they are delicious, but extremely filling, so be warned.

100 g • 4 oz sesame seeds

4 generous tablespoons honey

Put the seeds with the honey in a pan and simmer them gently for between 10 and 20 minutes, stirring every now and then. The mixture should turn a rich gold. To test whether it is ready, drop a spoonful on a wet plate, leave it to cool for a minute or so, then squeeze it into a ball. If it holds its shape it is ready. Take the pan off the heat and allow it to cool, stirring it every few minutes. When the mixture is almost cold wet your hands thoroughly in cold water and roll spoonfuls of the mixture into little balls; as long as your hands are cool and wet it will not stick to you. The sweetmeats should be stored in individual sweet wrappers to prevent them gradually running into each other. Alternatively, store them in a flat tin or container and cut them into small squares to serve, like Turkish delight.

LEMON PRESERVES

In modern Greece no cook could contemplate a culinary operation without a good supply of lemons; classical Greek cooks felt very similarly about the citron, a fleshier and slightly milder cousin of the modern lemon. These preserves, whose repeated boiling brings their flavour close to the original citron, could be eaten on bread, as a jam, but are better speared on cocktail sticks or little forks and eaten with coffee or iced water.

6 large, thick skinned lemons

450 g • 1 lb sugar

600 ml • 1 pint • 2½ cups water

Lightly grate the surface of the lemons to remove some of the bitterness. Cut deeply through the peel (as for peeling an orange) and remove it carefully, then cut it into smallish triangles. Put the pieces into a pan of cold water and bring it slowly to the boil. As soon as it boils, drain the peel and repeat the process twice more to remove the bitterness from the peel. Cover the peel with a fourth lot of water, bring it to the boil and simmer it till the peel is tender; leave it to cool then drain and dry the peel. In a separate pan bring the sugar and water to the boil with the juice of 2 of the lemons. Boil it for 5 minutes, then add the lemon peel and continue to boil for a further 10 minutes. Remove from the heat and leave for 24 hours. Bring the mixture back to the boil and continue to cook till the syrup is ready to set – it will take around 20 minutes. Test it by dropping a little on a saucer to cool; if it holds its shape once cool it is done. Remove the peel from the heat, and allow to cool before storing. You will find that there is just enough syrup left to coat each piece generously.

ANCIENT EGYPT

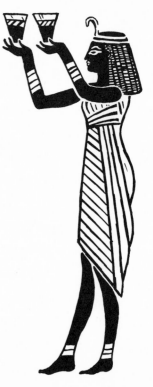

Egypt's history has always revolved round the great River Nile, the life staff of her people. It is in the flood plains of the Nile that the *melokhia* plant grows, whose leaves lend a rich and glutinous quality to one of Egypt's oldest dishes; it is the Nile's water which irrigates the fields of small brown fava beans for *ful medames*, the broad beans for *ta'amia* and *ful nabed* and the wheat to make the flat brown 'pocket' loaves which are eaten with everything.

The favourite dishes of the Egyptian people are also the simplest – and the oldest – their roots stretching as far back as the Pharaohs. Some, such as *batarekh* or dried mullet roe, are an acquired taste, although expatriate Egyptians will sell their souls for them; others, such as the flat bread pockets, very similar to what we know as pitta bread, have become universally popular. Flavourings are also simple; cumin, dried mint, dill, parsley, garlic and fresh lemon are the favourites. Even today, cooking apparatus often stretches no further than a single burner – in the old days it was an open fire – so, most dishes are best cooked long and slowly. A 'slow cooker' is ideal for these; alternatively, you can speed up the process by using a pressure cooker.

As in most Middle Eastern countries, desserts in the European sense scarcely exist, fresh fruits and nuts form a more 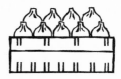 than acceptable substitute. However, over the centuries the taste for sweet confectionery has seeped through from further east and Egyptians delight in serving what we would call *petits fours*, rich with ground almonds, honey, sugar and nuts as a snack with coffee between meals.

An Egyptian meal would normally consist of a soup, then a fish or meat stew, bread, rice maybe, pickles and salads, followed by fresh fruit. The beloved bean dishes are eaten more as snacks or as light meals on their own.

MENU

MELOKHIA SOUP

BREADS

A FISH WITH TARATOR SAUCE
OR
FRIED FISH WITH COUSBAREIA SAUCE

FERIQUE

FRESH FRUIT & NUTS

MELOKHIA

SERVES SIX

Melokhia is one of the most ancient of Egyptian dishes, believed to be portrayed in Pharaonic tomb paintings, and the staple food of the Egyptian peasant from time immemorial. Each family has its own recipe for melokhia, whether as a soup or as a richer main dish filled with meats and other vegetables as it was in the middle ages. The fresh leaves (which look a bit like spinach) are seldom available outside Egypt but dried melokhia leaves can usually be found in Greek and Middle Eastern shops. If you wish to use this as a soup rather than as a main dish, reduce the quantity of meat by two thirds and leave out the rice.

1 kg • 2 lb lamb, chicken *or* duck
2 onions, chopped small
3 cloves garlic, crushed

salt and pepper
75 g • 3 oz dried melokhia leaves
6 large cloves garlic
2 tablespoons clarified butter *or* olive oil
2 tablespoons ground coriander
½ teaspoon chili *or* cayenne pepper
150 g • 6 oz patna *or* Basmati rice
3 extra onions, thinly sliced with 2 tablespoons
vinegar *optional*

Put the meat with the onion and garlic and a generous dose of salt and pepper in a large pan; pour in 1.8 litres • 3 pints water. Bring slowly to the boil, skimming any scum which may rise to the surface, and simmer for 2 hours. Remove the meat from the stock, discard any bones and chop it reasonably small. Strain the stock into a large, clean pan. If you want to serve the dish with rice, remove 600 ml • 1 pint of stock and use it to cook the rice; if it dries out add a little more, if there is too much liquid return it to the stock pot.

Crush the melokhia leaves with your hands or in a food processor. Bring the stock to the boil and add the melokhia leaves. Stir it well, bring back to the boil and simmer for 20 minutes.

Meanwhile crush the remaining garlic with a little salt and fry it carefully in the clarified butter or oil till it is golden. Add the coriander and the chili or cayenne powder and set aside till the soup is cooked. Return the meat to the pot along with the garlic sauce, boil together for a couple of minutes then serve in bowls with the rice. You can also garnish the dish with the onions, soaked in vinegar but I find the flavour rather too strong for the melokhia.

NB Do not overcook the melokhia leaves or they will refuse to stay suspended in the stock as they should.

FUL MEDAMES
(PRONOUNCED 'FOOL MEDA*MESS*')
SERVES SIX

Slowly cooked brown fava beans or ful is *the* national dish of Egypt and probably dates back to the Pharaohs. The beans are eaten by rich and poor, for breakfast, lunch and dinner, with bread, lentils, sauces, salads and, most frequently, eggs (see opposite). Traditionally the beans are cooked in an *idra*, a special earthenware pot tapering at the neck to reduce evaporation of the cooking water to a minimum, but any heavy pot with a well fitting lid will do. Seasoning (apart from the addition of some garlic once the beans are cooked) is done at the table.

750 g • 1½ lb dried ful *or* brown fava beans –
they are obtainable in most Greek or Middle
Eastern stores. You can also sometimes get the
beans tinned in which case you do not need to
soak or cook them.
2–4 cloves garlic crushed

Soak the rinsed beans for a minimum of 8 hours. Then put them in a large saucepan well covered with fresh water, bring to the boil, cover and simmer until they are tender but not mushy. This can take anything from 2–6 hours depending on how dry the beans were; if you have a slow cooker it can be used to cook the beans overnight. You can also cook them in a pressure cooker which reduces the cooking time to 30–45 minutes but remember that a microwave will *not* reduce the cooking time. When the beans are cooked, drain them and add the crushed garlic.

Serve the beans warm, in bowls, sprinkled with chopped parsley. Accompany them with oil or butter and lemon juice, salt, pepper, cumin and cayenne pepper or topped with Hamine eggs.

NB If you cannot get the proper ful use any dried broad bean as ful come from the broad bean family; the taste will not be totally Egyptian but a lot better than nothing.

HAMINE EGGS

These are eggs which have been very long and slowly cooked so that they are meltingly soft and creamy in the middle. They are used as a garnish for soups and stews but are most popular served with ful medames.

6 eggs

skins from several large onions *or* a tablespoon of ground coffee

Put the eggs with the onion skins or the coffee (I think the onion skins give a better flavour) in a large pan well covered with water and cook them on the lowest possible heat, or in a slow cooker, for at least 6 hours. Alternatively, if you are cooking ful medames, put the eggs (well scrubbed) and onion skins in with the beans to cook. Remove the eggs (remember to remove the onion skins also if you are cooking them in a pot of ful), shell them and serve them with the ful medames or in a stew or casserole (see Ferique Chicken, p. 46).

TA'AMIA *or* TAMEYA *or* BROAD BEAN RISSOLES
SERVES SIX

Ta'amia are one of the most traditional of Egyptian dishes, a favourite with the Christian Copts who are said to be the pure representatives of the ancient Egyptians. The rissoles should be made with dried broad beans which are very popular in southern Europe and usually to be found in Middle Eastern food shops. However, if you have difficulty locating them, the ta'amia are still excellent made with dried butter beans.

450 g • 1 lb dried broad beans, soaked for

24 hours and skinned

2 large onions, peeled and chopped

4 large cloves garlic

4 tablespoons chopped fresh coriander *or*

1 tablespoon ground

2 teaspoons ground cumin

½ teaspoon baking powder

generous shake of tabasco

1 teaspoon sea salt and plenty of freshly

ground black pepper

sesame or poppy seeds *optional*

oil for deep frying

Soak the beans for 24 hours, then pop them out of their skins and put them in a food processor with the onion, garlic, coriander, cumin, baking powder, tabasco, salt and pepper. Process *very* thoroughly till you have a smooth paste; if it is not smooth the patties will disintegrate in the cooking. If you do not have a processor use a liquidiser, in batches, or pound it by hand in a pestle and mortar – hard work, but how it would originally have been done. Set the purée aside for at least half an hour, then form it into flat round cakes 3–4 cm • 1–1½ inches across and coat them in sesame or poppy seeds. This is not necessary but I found it made the ta'amia even more delicious. Leave them aside for a further 15 minutes.

Heat the oil till a piece of bread dropped in it is well tanned in 1 minute. Gently let the rissoles down into the oil and deep fry them for 2–3 minutes or till they are nicely browned all over.

Remove from the oil, drain on kitchen paper towel and serve accompanied by fresh salads and breads.

NB You can also make the rissoles into small round balls and use them as cocktail snacks.

EGYPTIAN FISH WITH COUSBAREIA SAUCE★
SERVES SIX

Frying fish, whole or in slices, is a popular and traditional way of serving fish in Egypt. Almost any fish can be used and needs only lemon wedges to set it off, although a wide variety of local sauces are served. In this one the hazelnuts give an interesting texture and the pine nuts a wonderful flavour to the sauce.

approximately 1 kg • 2 lb of fish – red mullet is an Egyptian favourite and delicious, but expensive. Substitute any firm fleshed white fish.
flour.
clean oil for deep frying
2 onions, thinly sliced
2 tablespoons, olive oil
225 g • 8 oz tomatoes, sliced
100 g • 4 oz hazelnuts, coarsely chopped
50 g • 2 oz pine nuts
3 tablespoons finely chopped parsley
salt and black pepper

Clean the fish thoroughly; cut large fish into thick slices, and leave small fish whole. Dry them very thoroughly, then dredge them with flour. Meanwhile, heat the oil till it is very hot and gently lower the fish pieces into it; do not try to cook too many at the same time as the temperature of the oil must be kept as hot as possible to prevent them going soggy. The fish should take between 5 and 10 minutes to fry and should be light golden and crisp. Remove the pieces from the oil and drain them on kitchen paper. They can be served as they are with salt, pepper and lemon wedges; alternatively continue as below.

In a deep pan heat the oil and fry the onions till they are soft and just golden. Add the hazelnuts and pine nuts and fry for a couple of minutes more, then add the tomato slices and cook till they soften. Add just enough water to cover the vegetables, stir in the parsley, season to taste with salt and pepper and simmer for another few minutes. Carefully lay the fish pieces in the dish and spoon a little of the sauce over them. Cover the pan and simmer gently for 15 minutes. Alternatively, put the sauce with the fish pieces in an ovenproof dish and cook in a moderate oven (180°C • 350°F • Gas Mark 4) for 15 minutes. Serve warm with rice or new potatoes.

FISH WITH TARATOR SAUCE
SERVES SIX

A large fish, baked or barbecued, then ornately decorated with lemon slices, pine nuts, pickles, olives and radishes arranged in a complex oriental design, often forms the centre piece of a Middle Eastern grand dinner. The fish will be accompanied by bowls of tarator sauce which, according to taste and whether you find yourself in Egypt, Iran or Turkey, can be based on pine nuts, almonds or hazelnuts.

1 firm white fleshed fish large enough to serve 6,
cleaned but with its head and tail on
salt, pepper and olive oil
2 lemons
100 g • 4 oz pine nuts, almonds or hazelnuts
1 thick slice white bread without the crust
1–2 large cloves garlic
½ teaspoon salt

Rub the fish well with salt, pepper and olive oil, making a few slits in its skin so that the seasoning goes well in. Wrap it in foil with one of the lemons, sliced, and bake it in a moderate oven (180°C • 350°F • Gas Mark 4) for approximately 10 minutes to the pound or till the skin lifts easily off the flesh. Remove the fish carefully, reserving the juices. Skin and fillet it, keeping the head and tail and arrange the fillets on a serving dish. Replace the head and tail at the top and bottom and decorate the fish as ornately as you fancy with lemon slices, toasted pine nuts or slivered almonds, sliced olives, sliced pimento, sprigs of fresh coriander etc.

To make the sauce skin the nuts, if they are not already skinned (almond skins will pop off if soaked for 5 minutes in boiling water; hazelnuts are best toasted in the oven till the skins are brittle when you can rub them off). Then put them in a food processor or liquidiser with the slice of bread, the garlic cloves, the salt, the juice from the remaining lemon, the reserved fish juices and 150 ml • 5 fl oz of water. Blend until you have a fairly smooth sauce adding a little more water if the sauce is too thick, although it should be a thick coating consistency. Adjust the seasoning to taste and serve the sauce in bowls with the fish.

NB The sauce is also delicious served as a dressing for almost any vegetable, hot or cold.

FERIQUE *or* CHICKEN *or* VEAL COOKED WITH WHOLEWHEAT & EGGS
SERVES SIX

Recipes for meats cooked with wholewheat are to be found in medieval Arab cookery books and no doubt date from much earlier. Like so many Middle Eastern dishes this dish requires long, slow cooking to tenderise the ingredients and bring out their flavour. Although the process can be speeded up by using a pressure cooker I always feel one loses just a little in flavour. A slow cooker which can be left to bubble all night is ideal.

1 large chicken *or* 1 kg • 2 lb of knuckle of veal, boned

1 calf's foot (if available), blanched

some marrow bone pieces (if available)

2 tablespoons olive *or* sunflower oil

1 large onion, finely chopped

6 eggs in their shells, scrubbed

225 g • 8 oz wholewheat kernels, washed and soaked for up to 1 hour. If you cannot get wholewheat you can use cracked; it will cook more quickly than the wholewheat so may be slightly 'mushier' in the finished dish

1–2 teaspoons of turmeric

salt and pepper

Heat the oil in the bottom of a large saucepan just big enough to hold the ingredients, or in a slow cooker. Add the onion, soften slightly then add the meats, eggs, the wholewheat and the turmeric which will give the whole dish a lovely golden colour. Add enough water to cover fairly generously, cover the pan tightly and cook very gently for 3–4 hours. The meat should be very tender and falling off the bone, the wheat swollen and well cooked. Remove the meat and bones from the pan; carve the meat and discard the bones. Shell the eggs. Taste the soup/juices and season to taste. Serve the ferique – pieces of meat, eggs, wheat and juices – in deep bowls with extra salt, pepper and ground cumin. If you have liquid left over it makes delicious soup.

Sweet *petits fours*, usually based on ground almonds, are to be found all over the Middle East. In Egypt they are served to guests with coffee and iced water. Small bowls of exotic jams, eaten with a small silver spoon, are a bonus.

GLAZED WALNUTS★

MAKES APPROXIMATELY FIFTEEN

50 g • 2 oz ground almonds
50 g • 2 oz caster *or* superfine sugar
1–2 tablespoons orange blossom water
30 walnut halves
50 g • 2 oz sugar

Mix the almonds with the sugar and add sufficient orange blossom water to make a thick paste. Sandwich the walnut halves together with the almond paste and lay them on a cake rack. Melt the remaining sugar and cook it till it is light brown in colour; carefully pour this over the walnuts so that each is coated. As the caramel cools it will hold the walnut halves together.

DRIED FIG & APRICOT JAM★

MAKES APPROXIMATELY 1 KG • 2 LB

225 g • 8 oz dried figs, their stems removed
225 g • 8 oz dried apricots
225 g • 8 oz sugar
300 ml • 10 fl oz water
juice of ½ lemon
½ teaspoon aniseeds *optional*
2 tablespoons pine nuts
50 g • 2 oz chopped walnuts

Chop the figs and apricots roughly. Boil the sugar with the water and lemon juice for a minute or two till the sugar is well dissolved. Add the fruit and simmer gently for approximately 30 minutes or till the fruit is quite soft and the juices have thickened enough to coat the back of a spoon. Stir frequently to make sure it does not stick. Add the aniseeds (if you are using them), the pine nuts and the walnuts, stir thoroughly, cook for a further few minutes then pot the jam in warmed, well-cleaned jars with tight fitting lids.

NB The jam can also be used spread on bread if you prefer.

IMPERIAL ROME

Rome is the only one of the ancient civilisations from which we are lucky enough to have a 'real, live' recipe book. It is attributed to a certain Apicius although it is not at all sure that this slightly jumbled 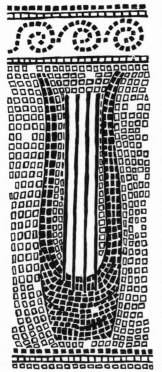 and repetitive, but fascinating compilation of recipes was not dedicated to Apicius rather than assembled by him. There were at least two gentlemen of that name who lived in Rome in the last century BC both of whom had great reputations as gastronomes, and to both of whom aspiring chefs would have been only too eager to dedicate a collection of recipes. The 'editions' of Apicius which have come down to us date from the third century AD but are obviously based on much earlier collections so could easily trace their origin back to the great days of the Republic.

In any case, whatever its origin, we are extremely lucky to have it and all the recipes to be found in this section have been drawn from it.

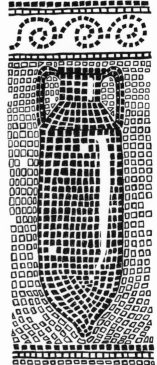

What is surprising about Apicius' book is how similar the dishes he suggests are to many modern Italian recipes; how simple the majority of them are – and how good. The tales of gluttony, the feasts of Trimalchio, the vomitoriums and the excesses of a Nero or a Heliogabalus are obviously only the 'lurid insanities of a declining civilisation'; the Romans for whom Apicius' book was written ate well but restrainedly making use of quite commonplace ingredients to create delicious, well balanced and healthy food.

As one would expect from southern Italy, the vegetables are plentiful and used in a wide number of ways. Seafood from the Mediterranean was popular, poultry, game, pork and offal equally so but there is relatively little beef or lamb. Wine was used extensively both in the cooking and to accompany the meals, oil was the main cooking fat, honey the main sweetener. Pepper, fresh coriander,

MENU

MUSHROOMS STEWED IN WINE
WITH CORIANDER

FLAT WHOLEMEAL BREADS
PITTA BREAD

BAIAN FISH STEW

FIGPECKERS OR POUSSIN WITH
ASPARAGUS SAUCE

SALADS

A COMPOTE OF UNRIPE FRUIT

thyme, rue, savoury, fennel and oregano were all used constantly, as was vinegar to give piquancy to dishes both sweet and savoury. As in all southern Europe, 'puddings' were seldom made, fresh or dried fruits forming the dessert course of nearly every meal.

Romans ate from low tables, lying on cushions  and leaning on their elbows. Authentic though it would be to serve a Roman meal that way, your guests might be more comfortable sitting and eating conventionally!

MUSHROOMS STEWED WITH CORIANDER & RED WINE
SERVES SIX

Serve the mushrooms in ramikin dishes as a starter with fresh brown bread. Alternatively you could use it as a summer salad or even as a cocktail snack, each mushroom speared on a cocktail stick. The fresh coriander is very typical of ancient Roman cooking; if you cannot obtain the herb fresh the dish is still worth making with dried, if you can find it.

600 ml • 1 pint • 2½ cups red wine

500 g • 1¼ lbs button mushrooms

salt and freshly ground black pepper

3 tablespoons of chopped fresh coriander *or*

2 tablespoons of dried

Put the wine in a pan, bring it to the boil and boil briskly till it is reduced to 450 ml • 15 fl oz • 2 cups. Wipe the mushrooms and remove their stalks. Add them to the wine with a pinch of salt and a generous grind of black pepper. Bring the wine back to the boil and simmer gently for 5 minutes. Remove the pan from the heat. If you are using dried coriander, add it to the mushrooms immediately, adjust the seasoning to taste and allow them to cool. If you are using the fresh herb do not add it to the mushrooms till just before you want to serve them. They are equally good warm or cold.

BEETS WITH LEEK & CORIANDER

SERVES SIX

An excellent Apician dish which will serve equally well hot as a vegetable or cold as a salad.

1 kg • 2 lbs fresh young beetroots (beets) scrubbed and thickly sliced
450 g • 1 lb trimmed leeks, thickly sliced
1 teaspoon ground cummin
1 tablespoon chopped fresh coriander *or* 1 teaspoon ground
600 ml • 20 fl oz • 2½ cups sweet white wine *or* medium *or* dry white wine sweetened with 1–2 tablespoons honey
salt and pepper

Put the beets with the leeks and the spices in a heavy bottomed pan or a microwave dish. Add the wine or wine and honey mixed, bring to the boil and simmer for 30 minutes or till the beets are tender. Alternatively cook them in a microwave for approximately 10 minutes. Season to taste with salt and pepper and serve either hot or cold.

A PURÉE OF LENTILS & CHESTNUTS

SERVES SIX AS A STARTER OR VEGETABLE OR FOUR AS MAIN COURSE

A mixture of two 'formulae' from Apicius' cook book, this makes a very flexible, filling, and delicious vegetable dish to be served warm or cold.

225 g • 8 oz cooked chestnuts, fresh or tinned
2 grinds of pepper and a generous pinch of cumin
1 level teaspoon coriander seeds
1 teaspoon fresh, chopped mint *or* ½ teaspoon dried mint
1 teaspoon wine vinegar
1 tablespoon olive oil
90 ml • 3 fl oz • ⅓ cup vegetable or meat stock, water *or* water and wine
350 g • 12 oz red lentils
2 medium leeks, peeled and sliced thinly
1 teaspoon crushed coriander seeds
1 tablespoon chopped fresh coriander leaf *or* 1 teaspoon dried

½ tablespoon fresh chopped mint *or*

½ teaspoon dried

1 teaspoons *each* red wine vinegar and honey

150 ml • 5 fl oz • ⅔ cup white wine

750 ml • 25 fl oz • 3 cups vegetable or meat stock

salt

TO DECORATE

fresh chopped coriander, toasted sunflower or

sesame seeds

Put the chestnuts in a pan with the pepper, cumin, coriander seeds, mint, oil, vinegar and stock; bring to the boil and simmer for 10 minutes. Purée in a liquidiser, processor or sieve. Meanwhile put the lentils in a deep pan with the leeks, coriander seeds and leaves, mint, vinegar, honey, wine and stock; bring to the boil and simmer for approximately 20 minutes or till the lentils are cooked and have absorbed the liquid. Mix the chestnut purée into the lentils and season to taste with salt. Turn into a serving dish and decorate with the chopped coriander or the seeds. Serve warm or cold, but not chilled.

A 'LAXATIVE' DISH OF CELERY & LEEKS

SERVES SIX

It is not clear why Apicius calls this a 'laxative' dish since he suggests a wide range of other vegetable dishes with no such warning. It does not appear to have any alarming effects on twentieth-century stomachs!

2 small heads of celery, sliced roughly

6 medium leeks,

trimmed and thickly sliced

25 g • 1 oz butter

salt and freshly ground black pepper

Put the celery in a pan just covered with water; bring it to the boil and simmer it for 10–15 minutes (approximately 5 minutes in a microwave) or till it is cooked but still slightly crunchy. Drain the celery but reserve the cooking water. Meanwhile cook the leeks briskly, uncovered, in enough water to cover them generously, until they are almost mushy and the water reduced by approximately one third. Drain them and reserve their water also; mix this with the celery water.

Mix the celery with the leeks and turn them both into a serving dish; cover and keep warm. Melt the butter in a pan and add 300 ml • 10 fl oz • 1¼ cups of the vegetable water (the rest can be used in soup); cook it together for a couple of minutes and season lightly. Pour over the vegetables and serve at once.

BAKED CABBAGE WITH CRACKED WHEAT & PINE NUTS

SERVES FOUR AS A MAIN COURSE OR SIX AS A VEGETABLE

An excellent vegetarian dish served by itself or a filling accompaniment to a plain roast or casseroled meat. If you find the mixture of cabbage, wheat, raisins and nuts altogether too exotic, you can leave out the raisins without spoiling the dish. The pine nuts though were great Roman favourites so should be retained.

450 g • 1 lb white *or* green cabbage, finely sliced

1 onion, finely sliced

15 g • ½ oz butter

150 ml • 5 fl oz • ⅔ cup vegetable *or* chicken

stock

salt and pepper

100 g • 4 oz cracked wheat

120 ml • 4 fl oz • ½ cup white wine

240 ml • 8 fl oz • 1 cup boiling water

50 g • 2 oz pine nuts

50 g • 2 oz raisins

25 g • 1 oz butter

Cook the finely sliced onion gently in the butter till it is transparent. Add the cabbage, mix the onion well in then add the stock and a little seasoning. Cover the pan and simmer gently for approximately 15 minutes or till the cabbage is cooked but still slightly crunchy; it can also be cooked in a microwave for approximately 5 minutes on high. Turn the cabbage into an oven proof dish. While the cabbage is cooking, put the cracked wheat into a bowl and pour on the boiling water followed by the wine. When the wheat has swelled and absorbed all the liquid, stir in the pine nuts and the raisins. Spread the mixture over the cabbage in the dish and dot the top with butter. Cook in a moderate oven (180°C • 350°F • Gas Mark 4) for 20 minutes and serve at once.

COLD BREAST OF POUSSIN WITH ASPARAGUS SAUCE
SERVES SIX

In the original of this recipe Apicius used whole 'figpeckers', small birds who still peck at the fruit on the fig trees of southern Italy. Since the idea of eating song birds whole is not one that appeals in the twentieth century I have substituted small poussin or guinea fowl, but kept the rest of the recipe intact.

1 kg • 2 lb trimmed asparagus

6 poussins *or* guinea fowl

300 ml • 10 fl oz • 2¼ cups white wine

6 shallots, peeled and sliced

2 bay leaves

1–2 teaspoons honey

6 egg yolks

salt and pepper

Put the trimmed asparagus in a deep pot with 1.2 litres • 2 pints • 5 cups of water. Cover with a lid which does not touch the tips or with a foil hood, bring to the boil and simmer for approximately 20 minutes or till the asparagus is tender. Remove 6–8 tips with care and reserve for decoration; remove the rest of the asparagus and set it aside. Pour the cooking water into one or two pans large enough to hold the poussins or guinea fowl, add the birds, then the wine, chopped shallots and bay leaves. Cover the pans, bring them to the boil and simmer for 45 minutes or till the birds are cooked. Remove the birds from the pots and cool sufficiently to be able to handle them. Skin and remove the breasts and lay them out on a dish; the rest of the birds can be used for another dish, soup etc. Cover and set aside to cool completely.

Meanwhile, purée the asparagus with 300 ml • 10 fl oz • 1¼ cups of the cooking juices and transfer it to the top of a double boiler. Heat gradually, then add the egg yolks. Continue to heat, stirring continually, till the sauce thickens slightly then add the honey, salt and pepper to taste. If the sauce is too strong or too thick, add a little more of the cooking juices. When you are happy with the flavour and texture, spoon it over the poussin breasts and garnish the dish with the asparagus tips. Serve lightly chilled with rice or small new potatoes and a really good green or spinach salad.

AN APICIAN BAKED HAM

There is an inscription on the wall of an inn in Pompeii to the effect that the innkeeper's clients would lick the saucepans in which his hams were cooked; who can say whether he too used this method but it is certainly good enough to lick.

2 kg • 3–4 lb joint of gammon, soaked for a minimum of 2 hrs if you suspect it of being salty, or overnight if very salty

15 large dried figs

6 bayleaves

1 tablespoon honey

350 g • 6 oz wholemeal/wholewheat flour

2 tablespoons olive oil

Put the gammon with the figs and bay leaves in a large pot and cover with water. Bring to the boil and simmer for approximately 20 minutes to the 500 g • 1 lb. While the meat is cooking make the pastry by stirring the oil into the flour then mixing to a soft dough with the cold water; set aside. Remove the joint from the water and peel off the skin. Cut this into small squares and put them to soak in 1 tablespoon honey melted in 2 tablespoons of the cooking liquid.

Allow the meat to cool slightly then roll out the pastry and cover the joint tucking the pastry in around its bottom. Transfer to a baking sheet and bake in a moderate oven (180°C • 350°F • Gas Mark 4) for 30 minutes or till the pastry is cooked. 10 minutes before it is ready take the joint out of the oven and stick the pieces of skin all over it, holding them in place with cocktail sticks; return to the oven to finish.

Meanwhile, remove the figs from the cooking juices and reserve. Take 60 ml • 20 fl oz • 2½ cups of the cooking liquid, add the honey mixture the skin was soaked in, and boil it fast to reduce it to 450 ml • 15 fl oz • 1⅞ cups. The ham can be served hot or cold accompanied by the figs and the reduced cooking juices. If it is to be served cold the juices should be chilled so that any excess fat can be removed before they are served.

SOLE IN WHITE WINE WITH HERBS

SERVES SIX

Whatever doubts one may have about the delicacy of ancient Roman palates will be dispelled by Apicius' fresh and simple recipe for sole.

6 small lemon soles *or* 3 large ones cleaned but
not filletted unless you really cannot bear
the idea of boning the fish yourself
2 tablespoons olive *or* sunflower oil
6 small leeks (*or* 3 large ones) trimmed and
very finely sliced
6 sprigs of fresh coriander, roughly chopped. If
you cannot find any fresh coriander use
3 teaspoons of dried although the flavour
will not be quite so good
300 ml • 10 fl oz • 1¼ cups dry white wine
6 grinds of pepper and a generous pinch of salt
1 teaspoon chopped fresh mint *or* lovage *or*
½ teaspoon of dried
1 teaspoon dried oregano
2 egg yolks

Pour the oil into the bottom of a wide heavy based pan or a microwave dish. Lay the fish on top and sprinkle the leeks and chopped coriander over it. Pour in the wine, cover the pan or dish and cook over a very low heat for 15–20 minutes or in a microwave for 5–8 minutes; the fish should be translucent but not disintegrating. Carefully remove the fish from the pan, leaving the leeks, herbs and juices. Remove the black skin and fillet the fish; lay the fillets on a warmed serving dish, cover them tightly and keep them warm. Add the salt and pepper, lovage or mint and the oregano to the pan juices. Stir in the egg yolks and cook over a *very* low heat till the sauce thickens slightly. Adjust the seasoning to taste and spoon the sauce over the fish. Serve at once with hot brown rice.

A BAIAN SEAFOOD STEW
SERVES FOUR–SIX AS A MAIN COURSE, SIX–EIGHT
AS A SOUP

Baiae was a popular seaside resort near Naples which is presumably where Apicius tasted this delicious fish soup/stew. The original suggests 'sea nettles' which I have interpreted as a seaweed; I used *kombu*, a dried Japanese seaweed, which worked well and is reasonably easy to obtain. If you cannot find it, do not worry, the stew is still excellent without it.

2 tablespoons olive oil

1 stick celery, chopped very small

6 grinds fresh black pepper

½ teaspoon ground cumin

1 tablespoon chopped fresh coriander *or*

1 teaspoon dried

10 g • ½ oz dried *kombu or* other dried seaweed, chopped small

1 small sprig fresh rue, if obtainable

300 ml • 10 fl oz • 1¼ cups medium white wine

1 kg • 2 lbs *very* well washed fresh mussels in their shells or 350 g • 12 oz frozen (the flavour is not as good but still worth making)

900 ml • 1½ pints • 3¾ cups water

3–4 fresh or frozen scallops, chopped small

25 g • 1 oz pine nuts, lightly browned in the oven or under a grill/broiler

Heat the oil in a large pan and gently cook the celery, pepper, cumin and coriander till the celery has softened. Add the seaweed, rue and white wine, bring to the boil and simmer for a couple of minutes. Bring up to a fast boil, add the fresh mussels, put on a lid and cook them for 3–5 minutes over a high heat till the shells have all opened – discard any that do not. If you are using frozen mussels add them to the wine and gradually bring the pot back to the simmer.

Add the water, bring back to the boil and simmer for 10 minutes. Remove the sprig of rue then remove the mussels from their shells and return them to the soup pot. Add the chopped scallop and the pine nuts and continue to cook for a couple of minutes just to cook the scallops. Season to taste with salt if you need to (I do not find that it is necessary) and serve at once. Take care not to scrape the bottom of the pot in case you didn't get all the sand out of the mussels.

A COMPOTE OF EARLY FRUIT
SERVES SIX

Apicius recommends 'hard-skinned early fruits' for his compote, which I have interpreted as apples and pears, but I see no reason why the recipe should not work for other fruits especially if they are rather underripe. The Romans had access to wonderful soft fruits for much of the year and rightly judged them too good *au naturel* to wish to eat them any other way. Do not be put off by the vinegar; it gives a piquancy to the finished dish which is delicious.

3 small apples and 3 small pears, peeled, cored and sliced

½ teaspoon freshly ground black pepper

1 tablespoon fresh chopped mint *or*

1 teaspoon dried mint

2–3 tablespoons honey (depending on the sharpness of the fruit)

1 tablespoon red wine *or* cider vinegar

90 ml • 3 fl oz • ⅓ cup *each* medium white wine and water

Put the sliced fruit in a flat pan (if it is not to be cooked immediately store the slices in some acidulated water to prevent them turning brown). Sprinkle over the pepper and mint. Melt the honey with the vinegar, wine and water and pour the mixture over the fruit. Bring to the boil and simmer gently for 10–15 minutes or till the fruit is cooked without being mushy; transfer to a serving dish and serve either warm or cold with or without cream or yoghourt.

A BAKED DISH OF PEARS
SERVES SIX

Many of the fruit dishes which appear in Apicius use pepper to season the fruit. To frequent travellers in Italy or France, where black pepper is often used to point up the cool juiciness of fresh fruit, this will not come as a shock.

3 large *or* 6 small ripe pears, peeled, cored, quartered and sliced

3 grinds fresh black pepper

2 generous pinches ground cumin

1 tablespoon honey

30 ml • 2 fl oz • ¼ cup sweet white wine

4 eggs

Stew the pear slices, with the pepper, cumin, honey and wine, slowly on a hob for 10–15 minutes or till the pears are cooked but still slightly crunchy. Alternatively they can be cooked in a microwave for 3–5 minutes. Remove the pears from the cooking juices and dry them on kitchen paper then lay them out in a shallow oven proof dish. Beat the two eggs with a fork then beat in the slightly cooled cooking juices from the pears. Pour the mixture over the pears in the dish and bake them in a cool oven (160°C • 325°F • Gas Mark 3) for 20 minutes or till the custard is just set; it should take approximately 5 minutes in a microwave. Serve the pears warm or cold, with cream or yoghourt if you want although I feel they scarcely need it.

ANGLO-SAXON BRITAIN

We know relatively little about the Anglo-Saxon world which existed in Britain between the fall of the Roman Empire and the arrival of William the Conqueror in 1066, which is why the discoveries at Sutton Hoo (the results of which are housed in the British Museum) and the archaeological investigations at West Stow in Suffolk are so valuable.

Although the burial mounds at Sutton Hoo revealed silver and jewellery from as far afield as Greece and the Middle East such internationalism would have been restricted to the high kings and the governing lords. The Anglo-Saxon peasants in their straggling villages are unlikely to have had many contacts outside their immediate neighbourhood. This meant that, like their counterparts around Europe, they were restricted to what they could grow or catch in the ten miles around their village. In the case of West Stow this

would have been barley with some rye, oats and a little wheat in good years, carrot and turnips, onions, left behind by the Romans, wild garlic and many herbs; nuts, apples and pears, grapes which in a warm year could be made into wine but in a bad year would be turned into verjuice or vinegar, and wild berry fruits from the woods.

West Stow would have been well-provided with fresh fish from the many local streams in East Anglia or even from the North Sea. Hens were kept but mainly for eggs, so would seldom be eaten. Cattle and sheep were killed for food although their main use lay in providing milk for butter and cheese and wool for clothes. Pigs foraged in the woods and could be turned into excellent salt pork and brawn. Deer and wild boar-hunting was, theoretically, reserved for lordly folk but hares, pigeon, ducks, geese and all the birds that roam the flats of East Anglia were there for the village people to catch if they could.

MENU

GRIDDLED TROUT WITH HERBS

HARE OR RABBIT STEW WITH BARLEY

HONEY & HAZELNUT CRUMBLE

Cooking was done over a log fire on spits or in an iron cauldron suspended from a hook in the roof. Baking was normally on a stone in the fire covered by a clay pot. 'Cutlery' was restricted to a knife and a shallow bone spoon so eating was done mainly with the fingers and by dipping hunks of bread in the juices of the pot; soups were drunk straight from wooden bowls. Drinks were ale, milk and, on special occasions, mead.

An Anglo-Saxon meal would be best served outside, round a log fire on a pleasant evening, when fingers can be wiped on the grass and the fresh flavours of the herbs will taste particularly good.

GRIDDLED TROUT WITH HERBS
SERVES SIX

The most popular way of cooking fish fourteen hundred years ago is still heavily in favour today – spit cooking or barbecuing over an open fire. As anyone who has used a barbecue will know, the better the logs that make the fire and the more herbs, spices and juices used to baste the fish the better its flavour will be. The herbs below are what might have been used in Anglo-Saxon East Anglia but feel free to include any others you fancy; try to use fresh if you can although dried are quite acceptable.

6 fresh, cleaned trout
6 sprigs of fresh rosemary *or* 1–2 tablespoons dried
75 g • 3 oz soft butter

18 fresh mint leaves *or* 2 teaspoons dried
leaves from 6 sprigs fresh thyme *or* 2 teaspoons dried
6 fresh sage leaves *or* 1 scant teaspoon dried
1–2 teaspoons coarse sea salt
6–9 grinds black pepper

Put one sprig or a generous shake of rosemary down the middle of each fish. Chop all the other herbs and seasonings and mash them into the soft butter. Use this to coat the fish generously on each side. Griddle, barbecue or grill it for 4–5 minutes on each side or till the skin is well browned and the the flesh flaking off the bone. Baste now and then with the butter which runs off. Serve at once with lots of fresh bread and a salad or a simple green vegetable.

NB If neither spit nor barbecue are available, use a grill.

CARP IN NETTLE BROTH
or ANY OTHER FRESH WATER FISH
SERVES SIX

Carp is one of the oldest of fresh water fish; young nettle tops a favourite herb used in spring time to help 'clean out the system'. The Anglo-Saxons would have cooked their fish in a large cauldron hanging over the open fire and would have included much more broth than I am so that it could serve as a soup and a main meal. If you are using carp, soak it for a couple of hours in water with two tablespoons of vinegar to remove any muddiness.

2–3 carp, depending on size *or* enough of any other fresh water fish to feed 6, cleaned but with the head and tail left on

2 medium leeks, finely chopped

3 young nettle tops, finely chopped

1 sprig of rosemary *or*

1 teaspoon dried rosemary leaves

3 lovage leaves, if available, chopped small

1 large, tart eating apple, peeled and sliced fairly small

1½ tablespoons white wine vinegar

9 pepper corns and ½ teaspoon of sea salt

Put the cleaned fish in a dish just large enough to hold them and sprinkle over all the other ingredients. Add enough water just to cover the fish, put a lid on the pan, bring it to the boil and simmer it very gently for 10–15 minutes (you could also cook it in a microwave in which case it would take 4–5 minutes). When cooked the flesh should flake easily from the bone. Remove the fish carefully from the pan. Skin, bone and fillet them and return the fillets to the juices. Reheat gently before serving. Anglo-Saxons would have eaten the fish as a soup with bread or barley added to the broth; I serve it with new potatoes or rice.

HARE, RABBIT, VEAL *or* CHICKEN STEW WITH HERBS & BARLEY

SERVES SIX

Herbs are sadly under-utilised today – in seventh-century England they were one of the few flavourings available to the cook so were not to be lightly set aside. An Anglo-Saxon would have caught his hare (rabbits are thought to have arrived after the Norman conquest in 1066) in the fields around his village and made vinegar out of the wine which failed to mature to a drinkable state. Hares are rather specialised creatures these days but rabbit joints are fairly easy to obtain. If you have difficulty in finding either of them, the recipe will work well with stewing veal or chicken joints.

50 g • 2 oz butter
1–1.5 kg • 2–3 lb (depending on the amount of bone) of hare *or* rabbit joints, stewing veal *or* chicken joints
450 g •1 lb washed and trimmed leeks, thickly sliced
4 cloves garlic, chopped finely
175 g • 6 oz pot barley (obtainable in health food shops)
900 ml • 30 fl oz • 3¾ cups water
3 generous tablespoons red *or* white wine vinegar
2 bay leaves, salt and pepper
15 fresh, roughly chopped sage leaves *or* 1 tablespoon dried sage

Melt the butter in a heavy pan and fry the meat with the leeks and garlic till the vegetables are slightly softened and the meat lightly browned. Add the barley, water, vinegar, bay leaves and seasoning. Bring the pot to the boil, cover it and simmer gently for 1–1½ hours or till the meat is really tender and ready to fall from the bone. Add the sage and continue to cook for several minutes. Adjust the seasoning to taste and serve in bowls – the barley will serve as a vegetable.

SMALL BIRD & BACON STEW WITH WALNUTS *or* HAZELNUTS

SERVES SIX

Birds of all kinds are prolific in East Anglia and could survive harsh weather well enough to be available all year round. Hazelnuts and walnuts grew in abundance and kept well, so, even when there was no pig for bacon, or the weather had been too dry for fungi, a reasonable stew could still be made. With bacon and mushrooms as well, the stew could turn into a feast!

6 fatty rashers of bacon, chopped roughly
if you could not get fat bacon, 15 g • ½ oz lard *or* butter
3 cloves garlic, chopped finely
4 pigeons *or* other small game birds, 6 if they are very small
225 g • 8 oz mushrooms, whatever variety happens to be to hand, chopped roughly
75 g • 3 oz roughly chopped roasted hazelnuts *or* walnuts
300 ml • 10 fl oz • 1¼ cups real ale
150 ml • 5 fl oz • ¾ cup water
2 *or* 3 bay leaves
a little salt and freshly ground black pepper
6 slices coarse brown bread – fine textured breads go soggy

Fry the bacon, with the garlic, in its own fat till it is lightly browned in a heavy bottomed casserole. If the bacon was very lean add the lard with the pigeons and brown briskly on all sides. Add the mushrooms and nuts, continue to cook for a couple of minutes, then add the ale and water with the bay leaves.

Bring to the boil, cover and simmer very gently for 2–2½ hours – the birds should be falling off the bone. Remove the birds from the juices, cool the juices completely and remove any excess fat. The birds can be served whole on or off the bone. If the latter, carve them while they are cold then return them to the skimmed juices and reheat them gently. Adjust the seasoning to taste and serve either the whole birds or the slices on the pieces of bread, with plenty of the juices and 'bits'.

A good green salad to follow is the best accompaniment.

SUMMER FRUIT, HONEY & HAZELNUT CRUMBLE

SERVES SIX

Before the Norman Conquest far larger areas of the country were covered with lightly forested scrubland than today – a wonderful home for brambles and berry-bearing bushes – so, in the summer months, wild soft fruits would have been there for the picking. A baked dessert like this would have been sunk in the embers of the log fire with a cauldron or pot upturned over it to form a lid.

1 kg • 2½ lb mixed soft summer fruits –
raspberries, loganberries, strawberries, currants,
bilberries or whatever is available
honey *or* brown sugar to taste
75 g • 3 oz toasted hazelnuts
75 g • 3 oz wholemeal *or* wholewheat brown
breadcrumbs

Put the fruits in a pan or a microwave dish with about 20 cm • 1 inch water in the bottom and cook gently for 10–15 minutes (4–6 minutes in a microwave on high) or till the fruits are soft without being totally mushy. Sweeten to taste with honey or brown sugar (Anglo-Saxons would have used honey); how much you need will depend on what fruits you have used. Drain off the excess juice and save to serve with the pudding. Chop the hazelnuts in a processor or liquidiser until they are almost as fine as the breadcrumbs but not quite, then mix the two together. Spoon the fruit into an ovenproof dish and cover with a thick layer of the hazelnuts and crumbs. Bake in a moderate oven (180°C • 350°F • Gas Mark 4) for 20–30 minutes or till the top is slightly crunchy and browned. Serve with lots of cream or plain yoghourt and the warmed fruit juices.

STEAMED CARROT & BARLEY PUDDING
SERVES SIX

Sugar was unknown in seventh-century England so Anglo-Saxon cooks had to rely on honey, wild fruits and sweet vegetables like carrots for 'dessert' dishes. To 'steam' a pudding you could

sink a pottery or metal bowl in a cauldron of soup or stew, thus maximising the heat of the log fire. Barley was the main cereal crop in East Anglia so appeared in most dishes, sweet and savoury.

100 g • 4 oz pot barley (obtainable in most health food shops)

50 g • 2 oz carrots, scrubbed and chopped roughly

1 tablespoon honey

225 g • 8 oz peeled and chopped tart apple, cooking or eating

450 ml • 15 fl oz • 2 cups water

2 sprigs of fresh mint, chopped *or* 1 teaspoon dried

2 large eggs

4–6 tablespoons warmed crab apple, quince *or* redcurrant jelly

150 ml • 5 fl oz • ⅔ cup double cream *or* plain yoghourt to serve

Put the barley, carrots, honey and apple in a pan with the water, bring it to the boil and simmer uncovered for 20–30 minutes or till the barley has absorbed most of the water and is soft without being mushy. Purée the mixture in a food processor (an Anglo-Saxon would have used a pestle and mortar) with the mint. Beat the eggs and mix them into the pudding. Butter a pudding basin just large enough to hold the mixture with about 2 cm • 1 inch to spare at the top and pour in the mixture. Cover the bowl with greaseproof paper and tie it firmly around the lip. Steam in a saucepan with water about ⅔ of the way up the bowl for 45–50 minutes; the pudding should be risen and firm to the touch. Alternatively, cover the basin with clingfilm and cook in a microwave on high for 4 minutes. Unmould the pudding onto a warm plate and serve at once with the warmed fruit jelly and cream or yoghourt.

PRE-CONQUEST AMERICA

Approximately nine thousand years ago agriculture got underway in both the fertile crescent of the Middle East and in the Valley of Mexico. In Mexico it was peppers, pumpkins and avocados that our forefathers grew, followed in later centuries by corn and beans and then, further south in the Andean highlands, potatoes, sweet potatoes, cassava and, from further south still, peanuts. The lack of domesticated farm animals (with the exception of the llamas and alpacas of the highlands) for meat and dairy produce, encouraged the early southern American civilisations to develop rich, colourful and delicious ways with vegetables and spices, the taste for which lasts to this day.

Chicken, now the most popular of south American meats, was unknown before the Spanish conquest, but turkey, duck, quail, dove, pheasant and other game birds were cultivated by the Aztecs. Indeed the most famous of all Aztec dishes, the *Mole poblano de Guajolote*, is based on turkey cooked in a rich sauce of chili, nuts and seeds, flavoured with chocolate. Coastal regions abounded in fish whose flavours combined particularly well with the fiery heat of the chili pepper.

The arrival of the Spaniards with their European farm animals, their nuts, dried fruits and Far Eastern spices enormously enriched the cuisine as old was combined with new to create one of the most diverse culinary traditions in the world. In the twentieth century it is hard indeed to separate the old Mayan, Aztec or Inca elements out from the later colonial additions but each of the recipes here can trace its parentage to a pre-conquest dish.

Beans are the essential element in all Latin American cooking from Mexico to the southern tip of Chile. They come dried, in all colours and shapes, are cooked long and slowly and are then served either alone or as an accompaniment to almost any dish. Corn or maize breads of various kinds are made throughout the region. The most famous are the Mexican tortillas made from *masa harina*, a specially prepared corn meal, unhappily, not easy to find in Europe. The dough is flattened by hand or in a press and baked on a griddle but

MENU

PERUVIAN POTATOES WITH WALNUT & SHRIMP SAUCE

MOLE POBLANO DE GUAJOLOTE

FRIJOLES

SALADS

FRESH FRUITS

CAFE DE OLLA

should remain soft and moist; tortillas can be kept hot successfully for hours in a very low oven, wrapped in a napkin and foil. They can also be bought fresh or frozen in some healthfood shops and delicatessens.

As in so many of the warmer countries desserts have always consisted mainly of fresh fruits although the arrival of the Spaniards did spark off the development of dessert cooking rich in sugar and eggs. Chocolate was the indigenous drink of Mexico but beer and wine are now both popular and excellent thanks to the European immigrants of the last few centuries.

POTATOES & EGGS IN PIGEON & WALNUT SAUCE★

SERVES FOUR–SIX, DEPENDING ON APPETITES

A dish of 'potatoes with pigeon sauce', rather than 'pigeon with potato sauce' sounds odd to Europeans who think of potatoes purely as a rather bland accompaniment to a 'star attraction' meat dish. Not so the Incas who, rightly, valued the potato as wonderful food in its own right.

2 pigeons, approximately 225 g • 8 oz each

salt and freshly ground black pepper

3 medium sized onions

2 medium sized tomatoes

1 dried chili pepper, soaked in warm water to soften it

2 tablespoons olive oil

50 g • 2 oz broken walnuts

100 g • 4 oz fresh, low fat cream cheese

milk

4–6 eggs

1–1.5 kg • 2–3 lb scrubbed potatoes – you can either use small new potatoes whole or larger potatoes sliced or quartered

TO DECORATE

a little fresh parsley, watercress or coriander

Slice 2 of the onions and lay them in the bottom of a heavy based casserole. Split the pigeons and season them thoroughly on each side; lay them on top of the onions. Peel the tomatoes, slice them thinly and lay them on top of the pigeons. Cover the casserole with foil and then a lid and cook it over a *very* low heat, over an ovenproof mat if necessary, for 2–3 hours or till the pigeons are really tender. Give the casserole a shake now and then to make quite sure nothing is sticking. Let the pigeons cool in the casserole then remove them, bone them and chop the flesh coarsely. Strain the pan juices and reserve them – the vegetables make a beautiful base for a soup.

Cut the remaining onion into thick slices and fry gently in the oil until they are golden brown on each side; cool slightly. Put the onion, pigeon meat and pan juices into a food processor with the chili pepper (drained, deseeded and chopped), the walnuts and the cheese. Purée the mixture adding sufficient milk to reduce the consistency of the sauce to that of a thick mayonnaise.

Hardboil the eggs and cook the potatoes in a steamer or a microwave. Arrange the cooked potatoes, whole or sliced and the halved eggs, yolk side up, on a serving platter while they are still warm and pour over the sauce. Garnish the dish with chopped parsley, watercress or fresh coriander and serve it with a good green salad. You can also accompany it with fresh hot red peppers.

MERO EN MAC-CUM
or MAYAN FISH STEAKS
IN PEPPER & GARLIC SAUCE★
SERVES FOUR

The *annatto* flavouring of this dish is very typical of Mexican Mayan cuisine but unfortunately *annatto* is not at all easy to find. If you do not manage to locate it, leave it out rather than trying to substitute something else; the dish will still be excellent, just not quite so authentic.

1 kg • 2 lb of any firm fleshed white fish cut into
4 steaks
4 large cloves of garlic, crushed
¼ teaspoon cumin
½ teaspoon ground oregano
1 teaspoon ground *annatto*
salt and freshly ground black pepper
90 ml • 3 fl oz • ⅓ cup fresh orange juice
60 ml • 2 fl oz • ¼ cup fresh lime or lemon juice
1 fresh chili, green or red, seeded and
chopped *or* 1 dried chili, soaked in hot water,
deseeded and chopped

150 ml • 5 fl oz • ⅔ cup olive, sunflower *or*
corn oil
1 large onion, thinly sliced
2 cloves garlic, minced
2 tomatoes, sliced
2 medium sized red peppers, deseeded and
thinly sliced *or* 2 canned pimentos, cut in strips
2 tablespoons chopped parsley

Lay the fish steaks out on a dish then make a dressing of the garlic, spices, about 6 grinds of pepper and ½ teaspoon of salt mixed to a thin paste with the fruit juice. Coat the steaks on both sides with the marinade and leave them aside for at least 30 minutes.

To cook the fish, pour just enough oil into a shallow baking dish or wide pan to coat the bottom. Arrange the fish steaks with any spare marinade in the dish. Top the steaks with the fresh or dried chili, the onion, minced garlic, tomatoes and sliced peppers. Pour over the rest of the oil, cover the dish tightly and cook it on a low heat for 15–20 minutes or till the fish loses its translucent look; it can also be cooked in the microwave in which case it should take 5–8 minutes on high, depending on the thickness of the steaks. Sprinkle the fish with fresh parsley and serve at once with lots of hot rice.

OCOPA DE CAMARONES *or* PERUVIAN POTATOES WITH WALNUT & SHRIMP SAUCE★
SERVES FOUR

A delicious main dish for lunch or a light supper, easy to make with a food processor but laborious without. It can also be converted to a cheaper vegetarian dish by substituting 4 hard boiled eggs for the shrimps and decorating the finished result with black olives and pimentos.

4 medium sized potatoes, scrubbed
60 ml • 2 fl oz • ¼ cup of peanut *or* walnut oil – if they are not available, olive *or* sunflower oil will do perfectly well
1 small onion, sliced thickly
2 cloves garlic, finely chopped
3 dried chilis, deseeded and soaked in hot water for 30 minutes
50 g • 2 oz broken walnuts
50 g • 2 oz crumbly white cheese
225 g • 8 oz cooked shrimps or prawns, peeled
240 ml • 8 fl oz • 1 cup milk
salt

Steam or microwave the potatoes till cooked then halve them lengthways. Meanwhile, heat the oil and gently fry the onion and garlic over a low heat till the onion is golden. Put the oil, onions, garlic, chili, walnuts, cheese and 100 g • 4 oz of the shrimps or prawns in a food processor and purée, gradually adding the milk to reduce the consistency to a thick sauce. Add extra milk or oil if it seems too thick. Season to taste with salt. While the potatoes are still warm, lay them out on a serving dish, pour over the sauce and decorate with the remaining shrimp or prawns. The dish is best eaten when the potatoes are still just warm but if you want to prepare it ahead of time and eat it cold it is still excellent.

MAYAN CHICKEN AND PORK PIE
SERVES SIX

This recipe was inspired by an old Mayan dish from the Yucatán described by Elisabeth Lambert Ortiz as 'a corn pie wrapped in banana leaves'. Sadly many of the original ingredients are hard to find outside Mexico so I have adapted it to suit more conventional Western supermarkets.

2 large onions, roughly chopped

6 tomatoes, roughly chopped

6 large cloves garlic, roughly chopped

2 teaspoons dried oregano

2 tablespoons ground *annatto* if you can find it, if not substitute 1 tablespoon tandoori mix – it has a stronger flavour but is quite acceptable

½ teaspoon salt

350 g • 12 oz pork, trimmed and cubed

1 medium chicken, jointed

300 ml • 10 fl oz • 1¼ cups chicken stock

6 large tortillas

You can often find these fresh or frozen in delicatessens or healthfood stores; if all fails you may be able to get dried taco shells which, soaked for a few minutes in milk will make an acceptable, though not ideal, substitute. In the original recipe a dough is made with *masa harina*, a specially treated maize flour, and *annatto* oil.

Purée the onion, tomato, garlic, oregano, *annatto* or tandoori mix and salt in a processor or liquidiser. Lay the pork and chicken out in a heavy based pan or an ovenproof casserole and spoon over the purée. Pour on the chicken stock, bring to the boil, cover and simmer gently, on the hob or in the oven, for 45 minutes or till both meats are cooked. Remove the chicken from the pan, cool it slightly, bone it and return it to the mixture.

Lay out three of the tortillas in the bottom of a shallow dish just large enough to hold the mixture. Transfer the meat with some sauce onto the tortillas with a slotted spoon but leave the bulk of the sauce in the pan. Cover the meat with the remaining tortillas and reheat the mixture in a moderate oven till the tortillas on top are lightly crisped. Reheat the remaining sauce and serve it with the pie.

MOLE DE POBLANO
SERVES SIX

This must be Mexico's most famous dish, made with turkey for festive occasions, and for which there are literally dozens of recipes. However, two things they all share, both of which date its ancestry very firmly to the Aztec court of Moctezuma: the liberal use of chilis and the addition of a little plain chocolate, a food which was not only forbidden to women but reserved exclusively for royalty, the military nobility and the higher ranks of the priesthood.

The dish should be made with a combination of *ancho*, *mulato* and *pasilla* chilis but sadly such variety is seldom available in Europe. Although the depths of flavour is not as good, an acceptable *mole* can be made with any combination of chilis, dried or fresh, that you can lay hands on. For a special occasion, make larger quantities of the *mole* but use turkey rather than chicken. If possible, make the dish at least 24 hours before you need to use it to allow the flavours to mature.

2 small *or* 1 large chicken, jointed
2 onions and 3 cloves garlic

1 tablespoon lard
50 g • 2 oz *each* of *mulato* and *ancho* chilis
and 25 g • 1 oz *pasilla* chilis *or*
approximately 50–100 g • 2–4 oz of any chilis
you are able to find
(but remember that the shorter, thinner and greener they are the hotter their flavour is likely to be so treat them with circumspection)
2 medium onions
2 cloves garlic
6 tomatoes, chopped
50 g • 2 oz blanched almonds
50 g • 2 oz dry roast peanuts
50 g • 2 oz toasted sesame seeds
2 corn tortillas *or* slices of dry wholemeal *or* wholewheat toast
½ teaspoon *each* coriander and aniseeds
1 level teaspoon ground cinnamon
50 g • 2 oz dark chocolate
salt and pepper
1 teaspoon sugar *optional*

Put the chicken pieces in a pan with the onion and garlic, cover with water, bring to the boil and simmer for 30 minutes or till the chicken is almost cooked. Drain off and reserve the stock and dry the chicken pieces. Melt the lard in a heavy based pan and gently fry the chicken pieces on all sides till they are lightly tanned.

Meanwhile, remove the stems and seeds from the chilis, tear them up and soak the pieces in approximately 300 ml • 10 fl oz • 1¼ cups of boiling water for 30 minutes. Then, in a processor or liquidiser, purée the chilis with their water, the onion, garlic, tomatoes, nuts and seeds (reserving a few for decoration), spices, seasoning and chocolate. Remove the chicken pieces from the pan and pour off any excess fat. Fry the purée in the remaining lard for a few minutes, then add the meat with enough of the chicken stock for the sauce just to cover the meat, and continue to simmer gently for 30 minutes or till the chicken is thoroughly cooked. Ideally the *mole* should be put aside for at least 24 hours at this point to allow the flavours to develop. When you are ready to serve the *mole* reheat it, adjust the seasoning to taste and add a little sugar if you feel it is necessary. Serve it with plenty of tortillas, white rice, beans and guacamole sauce.

FRIJOLES *or* BEANS
SERVES SIX–EIGHT

Dried beans of one kind or another are, and always have been, absolutely essential to all south and central American cooking. Before the conquest they formed the main protein food of the Incas, Aztecs and highland Indians and even after the arrival of the Spaniards with their farmyard

animals and milk products, beans retained their central place at every meal. There are as many recipes for cooking them as days of the year but on the whole they are served as a side dish with a 'soupy' consistency, not used as a 'mopping up' vegetable the way they are in Europe.

450 g • 1 lb red kidney, black, pinto *or* pink
beans

4 large cloves garlic

2 bay leaves

1 tablespoon lard

1 onion, finely chopped

2 chilis, finely chopped *optional*

2 large tomatoes chopped small *or* 1 tablespoon
tomato paste

salt and pepper

Opinions differ as to whether the beans are better soaked overnight or precooked. If you remember, put the beans in a bowl or pan, generously covered in cold water (but *no* salt), and leave them overnight. If you do not, cover them generously in cold water in a pan, bring them to the boil and boil them fast for 10 minutes. Take them off the heat and allow them to stand for 1–2 hours. If the beans were soaked, put them, with their water into a pan with 2 of the garlic cloves, whole and spiked on a cocktail stick so that you can find them later. Bring them to the boil, add ½ tablespoon of lard and cook at a rolling boil for 1½–3 hours or till the beans are soft. If the water gets too low, add a little more boiling water. If they have been pre-cooked, add the garlic and lard and bring back to the boil adding more boiling water if it seems necessary and cook as above.

When the beans are soft, melt the rest of the lard in a heavy based pan and gently fry the other two cloves of garlic, chopped fine, the onion, the chilis if you want your beans hot, and the tomatoes or tomato paste. Add the beans with their liquid (having removed the garlic cloves on their cocktail sticks) and continue to cook for up to 30 minutes, mushing them into a rough purée or not as you prefer. Season the beans to taste before serving. If you can spare the time it is better to prepare them at least 24 hours before you need them as their flavour improves with keeping; indeed they will keep quite happily in the fridge for over a week.

COURGETTES *or* ZUCCHINI WITH A GREEN PEPPER SAUCE★

SERVES SIX

In Mexico this dish would be made with *poblano* chilis, a large, deep green pepper whose flavour varies from mild to quite hot. Elisabeth Lambert Ortiz suggests substituting sweet green peppers – and the results are quite delicious.

4 medium sized green peppers, toasted, skinned and deseeded

1 large onion, peeled and chopped

2 cloves garlic, chopped

3 tablespoons corn *or* sunflower oil

750 g • 1½ lbs young courgettes *or* zucchini wiped and cut into thick slices

salt and freshly ground black pepper to taste

5 tablespoons double cream *or* plain yoghourt

Toast the peppers by holding them, impaled on a fork, over a gas flame or an electric burner till they blister and blacken. Wrap them in a wet tea or dish cloth for 30 minutes then rinse them and peel off the skin under cold running water. It is not absolutely necessary to do this but the texture of the pepper is nicer and the flavour better if you do. Remove the seeds and ribs and chop the peppers coarsely. Purée them in a blender or processor with the onion and garlic. Heat the oil in a pan and sauté the purée, stirring continually, for 3–4 minutes. Add the sliced courgettes, season with salt and pepper and simmer till they are tender – 15 minutes should be enough. This can also be done in a microwave and should take no more than 5 minutes. Stir in the cream or yoghourt – if the latter remove the pan from the heat before adding the yoghourt or it will curdle – adjust the seasoning to taste and serve at once. It is delicious as a vegetable with any plainly cooked meat or fish.

AZTEC CHOCOLATE
SERVES SIX

Chocolate, or rather the cocoa bean from which the chocolate was made, not gold and silver, served the Aztec empire as money – to the infuriated disbelief of the Spanish invaders who found only rooms filled with cocoa beans where they expected to find chests of gold. Because it was so

valuable only emperors and the highest ranks in the land were allowed to drink this 'money'; when they did it was made with water, vanilla and honey since there was no milk. Modern Mexican chocolate always uses milk and sometimes eggs as well to turn it into a 'meal in one'.

350 g • 6 oz dark chocolate, broken up
1 litre • 36 fl oz • 4½ cups whole milk
½–1 teaspoon ground cinnamon
4–8 drops vanilla essence
3 eggs *optional*

Heat the milk with the chocolate, cinnamon and vanilla essence in a double boiler. Once the chocolate is melted transfer to a saucepan, bring to the boil then simmer, beating briskly with a balloon whisk or hand beater, for 2–3 minutes – simmering the milk gives a thicker mixture than merely warming it. Remove from the heat and carry on whisking till you have a good layer of foam. The chocolate can be drunk hot or cold but each mug should have a generous layer of bubbles. If you wish to add egg, do so after you have removed the chocolate from the heat and whisk it thoroughly.

CAFÉ DE OLLA
SERVES SIX

This is the most traditional way of serving coffee in Mexico. It can be made with already brewed coffee, the flavourings added after the coffee is made in case all guests do not like the sweetness, or brewed with the coffee.

1 litre • 35 fl oz • 4¼ cups brewed strong coffee
or water
If you are brewing the coffee, approximately
3 tablespoons (depending on the type) ground
coffee
5 tablespoons dark brown sugar
2 pieces cinnamon bark *or* 6 generous pinches
ground cinnamon
6 cloves

If you are brewing the coffee, combine the water with the other ingredients and bring them to the boil; add the coffee and continue as normal. If you are using ready brewed coffee, add the sugar, cinnamon and cloves to the brew, bring it back to the boil briefly, stir it well and serve. If you wish to serve the flavouring separately, bring the 5 tablespoons of water to the boil with the sugar, cinnamon and cloves. Simmer them for long enough to melt the sugar and serve with ready brewed strong black coffee.

MEDIEVAL EUROPE

In the last two centuries of the Middle Ages eating, among the upper classes at least, was a very Europeanised business. In England, France, Italy and the Holy Roman Empire ingredients were pounded and mashed, highly spiced, elaborately decorated and as exotic as the  means and the imagination of the cook could make them. Country folk on the other hand, made do as they always had, with what their patch of land could supply. And townsfolk, unless they happened to live in one of the few large ports where merchantmen docked with their holds laden with spices from the east, had little more choice than their country cousins.

Although we have many descriptions of grand medieval feasts we have very little in the way of cook books. *Le Viandier* compiled around 1380 by Guillaume Tirel or Taillevent, cook to the royal household of France for nearly fifty years, and *The Forme of Cury*, a collection of 196 recipes copied by Richard II of England's scribes at the dictation of his cooks around 1399, about complete the list. To what extent these recipes are 'original' to Taillevent or Richard's cooks rather than traditional dishes recorded for future use, we have no way of knowing. We do know however that the rich, expensive and elaborate dishes that they describe were restricted to the upper classes.

Meals were served in many courses, divided, rather vaguely, into meat and fish; fish only being served on the innumerable fast days and in religious houses. These courses could consist of up to twenty dishes including sweet concoctions along with the roasted birds, game and the occasional domestic animal. Vegetables and hard cheeses were seldom served as they were working-men's food. Bread though, appeared on all grand tables both in large, coarse slices known as trenchers which were used as plates, and as wastels or

MENU

A TART FOR EMBER DAY

A JELLIE OF FYSHE

SPIT-ROASTED MEAT WITH EGERDOUCE SAUCE

FENKEL IN SOPPES

A SALAT

A ROSY ALMOND CREAM

DATE AND GINGER LECHEMEAT & COMFITS

manchets which were finer wheaten rolls or buns. Guests were seated on one side only of long trestle tables down either side of a great hall (so they could get a good view of the evening's entertainment).

Each guest carried his own knife and spoon with him – forks were not yet in common usage. He was also provided with ample napkins with which to clean his hands in the basins of water brought round by servants after each course. Etiquette was strict and, despite the lack of eating implements, table manners were surprisingly refined.

As regards the food itself, the more exotic and unusual it could be persuaded to look the happier both cook and guests. Spices were used in large quantities both to colour and to flavour food which was often heavily salted and sometimes less than perfectly fresh. Dried fruits were also included for flavour, and sugar sprinkled as a spice on dishes both sweet and savoury. Exotic birds – peacocks, herons and swan – often formed the centrepiece to a grand display while courses were separated by immensely elaborate, and often inedible, sugar constructions designed to honour the most important guest of the evening.

A TART FOR EMBER DAY
SERVES SIX

An 'ember day' was one of the many days in the year on which the church forbade the eating of meat although dairy products, eggs and fish were allowed. The spices and raisins give the flan a very medieval flavour but if you do not fancy the sweetness just leave the raisins out.

250 g • 9 oz wholewheat *or* wholemeal pastry
(made with 150 g • 6 oz wholewheat *or*
wholemeal flour, 40 g • 1½ oz each of butter
and lard and a little cold water)
40 g • 1½ oz butter
150 g • 6 oz onions, roughly chopped
12 fresh sage leaves, chopped *or* 1 tablespoon of
dried sage
2 handfuls of fresh parsley, chopped roughly

75 g • 3 oz well flavoured cheese, grated
3 eggs
salt, pepper and ½ a teaspoon *each* ground
cinnamon and ginger
180 ml • 6 fl oz • ¾ cup milk
40 g • 1½ oz raisins *optional*

Make the pastry and line an 18–20 cm • 7–8 inch flan case; bake it blind.

Melt the butter in a pan and gently cook the onions with the sage and parsley until they are just soft. Add the cheese, eggs, seasoning and milk and mix well. Add the raisins if you are using them and pour the mixture into the flan case. Bake in a moderate oven (180°C • 350°F • Gas Mark 4) for approximately 20 minutes or till the tart is risen, firm and lightly browned. Serve warm or cold.

WASTELS YFARCED *or* TOASTED STUFFED BROWN ROLLS

SERVES SIX AS A STARTER, THREE AS A MAIN COURSE

Wastels were the good quality loaves served to the gentry at a late medieval feast. In this recipe, as in that for the 'lozenges' (see p. 98), the loaves were cooked in broth once they had been stuffed. Since I do not find soggy bread very attractive I have buried the filling in crisp brown rolls.

3 wholemeal *or* wholewheat brown rolls, halved

and with their crumb removed

50 g • 2 oz butter

100 g • 4 oz mushrooms, chopped roughly

100 g • 4 oz cooked and *very* well drained leaf

spinach, chopped roughly

50 g • 2 oz raisins

salt, pepper and ground cinnamon and

cloves to taste

1 large or 2 small eggs

Put the halved rolls in a moderately hot oven for approximately 10 minutes or till they are lightly browned and crisp.

Melt the butter in a pan and cook the mushrooms for a couple of minutes. Add the spinach and the raisins and continue to cook gently for several minutes or till the butter has been almost absorbed by the vegetables. Season to taste with the salt, pepper and spices. Beat the egg in a bowl, add it to the vegetable mixture and cook it gently just long enough for the egg slightly to bind the other ingredients. Pile the filling into the halved rolls and serve at once.

CAUDEL OF MUSCULS TO POTAGE
or BRAISED MUSSELS
SERVES SIX

This soup-cum-stew would have been served on one of the innumerable fish eating days which littered the medieval calendar and in a grand household would only have been one of ten or fifteen such dishes presented to the lord and his guests.

2 kg • 4½ lb fresh mussels *or* 750 g • 1½ lb frozen

2 tablespoons olive oil

1 large onion, very finely chopped

2 leeks, very finely sliced

40 g • 1½ oz ground almonds

2 teaspoons ground ginger

½ teaspoon *each* ground saffron, cloves, salt and 4 grinds of black pepper

450 ml • 15 fl oz • 2 cups milk

1–2 tablespoons white wine vinegar

If the mussels are fresh, clean them thoroughly, removing the beards and discarding any which do not close when tapped. Bring 5 cm • 1 inch water to the boil in the bottom of a large pan with a couple of slices of lemon and 150 ml • 5 fl oz • ⅔ cup of white wine. Drop the mussels in, turn the heat up to maximum, cover with a lid and cook briskly for 3–4 minutes or till all the mussels have opened. If any do not, discard them. Drain the remaining ones, remove them from their shells and reserve the juices. Meanwhile, cook the onion slowly in the oil till it is soft but not coloured. Put the leek with the almonds, spices and the milk in a pan or a microwave dish and bring to the boil. Simmer for a couple of minutes then add to the shelled mussels along with the onions. If you are using frozen mussels add them to the leek and onion mixture. Bring all to the boil and simmer together for a few minutes. Add the wine vinegar to taste and further seasoning if needed. Thin the sauce with some of the reserved cooking liquid if the mussels were fresh, with a little wine and water mixed if they were frozen, if you think it needs it. Serve the broth in bowls with plenty of fresh brown bread.

A JELLIE OF FYSHE
SERVES SIX

Elaborate and highly decorative jellies were the delight of the artistic medieval cook, often enhanced with edible gold and silver and enclosing whole fish or birds. These look wonderful but are rather impractical to eat, so I have restricted myself to whole scallops and whole prawns.

225 g • 8 oz hake, cod, haddock *or* other well-flavoured white fish

3 scallops

75 g • 3 oz prawns

2 onions, roughly sliced

1 tablespoon white wine vinegar

25 g • 1 oz ginger root, peeled and finely chopped

½ teaspoon sea salt and ¼ teaspoon white pepper

450 ml • 15 fl oz • 2 cups *each* white wine and water

20 g • ¾ oz gelatine

Put the white fish in a pan with the onions, vinegar, ginger root, spices, wine and water. Bring it gently to the boil and simmer for 10 minutes. Add the scallops and prawns and cook for a further 3 minutes. Remove the fish, bone and skin the white fish and set it all aside. Strain the cooking juices and set aside to cool for several hours by which time a lot of the sediment will have settled in the bottom of the bowl. Carefully pour off the juices, leaving the sediment, and then strain several times through a clean teacloth. You should have approximately 750 ml • 25 fl oz • 3 cups of liquid left. Melt 20 g • ¾ oz of gelatine in a little of the liquid, cool it to room temperature then mix it into the rest of the juices.

Pour a thin layer 1 cm • ½ inch of the juice into the bottom of a 1.2 litre • 2 pint • 5 cup soufflé dish or fish mould and put it in the fridge to set. Flake the white fish into smallish flakes; remove the coral from the scallops and cut the white flesh into three or four pieces. Once the jelly is firm, arrange the most decorative of the fish in the bottom of the dish – some scallop coral in the middle, prawns around the outsides, flakes of white fish in between or however you feel inspired. Spoon in a little more of the juice and return it to the fridge to set. Continue to layer the fish in the mould, setting each layer with a covering of juice until you have used up all the fish and juices. Leave the jelly to set for at least 4 hours in a fridge. Unmould and decorate with fresh herbs; serve as a starter or a light luncheon dish.

SPIT-ROASTED MEAT WITH EGERDOUCE SAUCE

In medieval Europe a fine joint of meat, be it venison, boar or bird, always deserved spit roasting over a huge open log fire. The spits were turned by kitchen boys or vagabonds who got a meal for their pains and the joints were periodically 'dusted' with spices and herbs. Since forks were still almost unknown the slices of meat were eaten in the fingers but accompanied by sauces. These were laid, in small dishes ('sauc-ers') along the tables, and diners would dip the little finger of the right hand only into the sauce to spread it on their meat. This finger was never licked but carefully wiped on a napkin out of respect for fellow diners.

In a modern kitchen any joint of meat can be used but it should be well flavoured if the egerdouce sauce is to be served with it. Cook it on a spit, a barbecue or, if you have neither, on an open rack in the oven. Sprinkle it with lightly ground mixed herbs plus a little of any spice that you fancy.

EGERDOUCE SAUCE
SERVES SIX

2 tablespoons olive oil

75 g • 3 oz onions, roughly chopped

25 g • 1 oz *each* raisins and currants

½ teaspoon *each* salt, ground ginger, mace and saffron

¼ teaspoon ground cloves

120 ml • 4 fl oz • ½ cup dry white wine

90 ml • 3 fl oz • ⅓ cup wine vinegar

25 g • 1 oz sugar

75 g • 3 oz wholemeal *or* wholewheat breadcrumbs

approximately 90 ml • 3 fl oz • ⅓ cup water

Gently cook the onions in the oil till they are soft. Add the fruit and spices and cook for a few minutes. Melt the sugar in the wine and vinegar and add this to the onion and fruits. Simmer all together, covered for 15 minutes then process or liquidise. Return the mixture to the pan and add the breadcrumbs and enough water to make a thick but not claggy sauce. Adjust the seasoning to taste and serve with the roast meat.

CRUSTADE OF CHICKEN & PIGEON
SERVES SIX

A 'crustade' usually involved a 'coffyn' or pastry case filled with meats, eggs and spices and then topped with another layer of pastry. Medieval cooks would have used a hot-water crust paste but I find that short crust is crisper and tastes better. If you want a slightly more twentieth-century flavour, double the quantity of chicken and leave out the pigeon, and substitute 25 g • 1 oz of bacon chopped and fried in its own fat for the raisins.

225 g • 8 oz–350 g • 12 oz wholemeal *or* wholewheat shortcrust pastry, depending on whether you want a lid on your crustade

1 pigeon

2 chicken joints (2 breasts *or* 2 whole legs)

150 ml • 5 fl oz • ⅔ cup dry white wine

several grinds of black pepper

4 cloves

15 g • ½ oz butter

50 g • 2 oz mushrooms, roughly chopped

25 g • 1 oz raisins

3 large eggs

salt, pepper and ½ teaspoon ground ginger

Roll out 225 g • 8 oz of the pastry and line a 20 cm • 8 inch flan dish; bake the crust blind.

Put the pigeon in a pot with the stock, wine, pepper and cloves and cook very slowly for an hour. Add the chicken and continue to cook for a further 45 minutes or till the meat of both birds is really tender. Meanwhile cook the mushrooms lightly in the butter. Remove the birds from the stock and bone them. Cut the flesh into quite small pieces, mix it with the mushrooms and the raisins and spread them over the base of the flan case.

Beat the eggs with a fork and season with the salt, pepper and ginger. Add 240 ml • 8 fl oz • 1 cup of the cooking juices and pour over the meat in the flan case. If you want it to have a lid, roll out the rest of the pastry and cover the flan. Bake it in a moderate oven (180°C • 350°F • Gas Mark 4) for 25 minutes if uncovered, 35 minutes if covered. Serve warm with a good green salad.

'FENKEL IN SOPPES'
or BRAISED FENNEL WITH GINGER
SERVES SIX

The original of this recipe comes from the *Forme of Cury*, the collection of 196 'receipts' copied by Richard II's scribes at his cooks' directions. To follow the original exactly the fennel should be served on 'soppes' or thick slices of coarse bread with the juices spooned over the top; you may prefer to use it without the bread just as a vegetable.

750 g • 1½ lb trimmed, fresh fennel root cleaned and cut in matchsticks

225 g • 8 oz onions, thickly sliced

1 heaped teaspoon of ground ginger

1 level teaspoon of powdered saffron

½ teaspoon salt

2 tablespoons olive oil

150 ml • 5 fl oz • ⅔ cup *each* dry white wine and water

6 thick slices of coarse wholewheat *or* wholemeal bread *optional*

Put the fennel in a wide, lidded pan with the onions. Sprinkle over the spices and salt, then the oil and finally pour over the liquids. Bring to the boil, cover and simmer for 20–30 minutes or till the fennel is cooked without being mushy. Stir once or twice during the cooking to make sure the spices get well distributed. Serve it alone with a roast meat or griddled fish or place one slice of bread on each warmed plate, cover it with the fennel and pour over the juices.

A SALAT
SERVES SIX

Salads, made mainly of herbs, were popular throughout the Middle Ages, often served at the start of a meal (as in twentieth-century America) rather than after the main course. The make up of the salad would change according to the season and what grew in each cook's herb garden, so feel free to adapt the basic recipe as you feel inclined. This is essentially a summer salad as its flavour depends entirely on the fresh herbs. Do not try to make it with dried herbs; you will only be disappointed.

2 bunches of watercress
2 cartons of mustard and cress
1 medium leek, very finely sliced
6 spring onions *or* scallions, chopped small
1 bulb of fennel, sliced in thin matchsticks
1 large handful of fresh parsley, pulled off into small sprigs
the leaves from 1 young sprig of fresh rosemary
the leaves from 4–6 sprigs of fresh mint, slightly chopped
6 fresh sage leaves, slightly chopped
the leaves from 2 small branches of thyme
a few leaves from any other herb you have growing in your window box *or* garden *or* find in the supermarket (take care not to use too much of any very strong flavoured ones) slightly chopped
sea salt and freshly ground black pepper
2–3 tablespoons wine vinegar
4–6 tablespoons olive oil

Wash the cresses, herbs and fennel and dry them all thoroughly. Mix them, with the leek and spring onions, in a large bowl, sprinkle with salt and pepper and mix again. Mix the oil with the vinegar and pour over the salad just before serving.

LOZENGES *or* CURD CHEESE PASTRIES

SERVES SIX

In the fifteenth-century version of this recipe the cooked pastry was 'seethed' or boiled 'in broth' before being layered with the cheese mixture. I have to admit to finding it one of the few occasions when the original did not prove as enticing as a modernised version. I have left the pastry crisp and made 'sandwiches' with the cheese mixture.

225 g • 8 oz wholemeal *or* wholewheat,

shortcrust pastry

225 g • 8 oz curd cheese

25 g • 1 oz very finely chopped stem *or*

crystallised ginger *or* plump raisins

15 g • ½ oz toasted and chopped pine nuts

sugar to taste

lemon juice to taste

Roll the pastry out very thin and cut it into small rectangles – approximately 15 × 8 cm • 6 × 3 inches – you should get at least 24. Bake them in a moderately hot oven (190°C • 375°F • Gas Mark 5) for ten minutes or till they are crisp and brown. Remove them and cool them on a rack.

Meanwhile mix the curd cheese with the ginger or raisins, the pine nuts and the sugar and lemon to taste. Set aside. When you are ready to serve them, sandwich together two pieces of pastry with the cheese mixture. They can be used as a dessert or as a snack.

A ROSY ALMOND CREAM
SERVES SIX

This looks very pretty served in glasses and decorated with a crystallised flower petal – which in medieval times would have been crystallised at home. Do not be too startled by the vinegar. It was used in ancient Rome, and is still popular in modern Italy, to emphasise the flavour of the fruit.

600 ml • 20 fl oz • 2½ cups milk

50 g • 2 oz ground almonds

40 g • 1½ rice flour

½ teaspoon ground cinnamon

1 teaspoon ground ginger

350 g • 12 oz berries or currants: raspberries,

blackberries, loganberries, red *or* black currants,

fresh, or frozen but defrosted

75 g • 3 oz sugar

1–2 tablespoons wine vinegar

crystallised petals to decorate

Put the milk in a pan or microwaveable jug with the ground almonds, bring them to the boil, and simmer for 3 minutes. Meanwhile, mix the spices with the rice flour in a pan, then gradually add the hot almond milk. Cook them together till the mixture thickens slightly. Add the fruit with the sugar. Cook them all together gently till the sugar is melted and the fruit well mixed – it should not totally disintegrate although it should be partially mushed. Add the vinegar to taste and spoon the dessert into glasses. Chill for a couple of hours but serve at room temperature, decorated with another berry or with a crystallised rose or violet petal.

CHARDEWARDEN, CHARDECRAB or CHARDEQUINCE

When sugar was hard to come by and the fruit season was short the best way to preserve excess fruit was to cook it immensely long and slowly till it turned into a sort of paste which would keep for several months; fruit cheeses are a modern day equivalent. You can use any hard fruit which is in abundance (pears, apples, quinces etc.), roll the resulting paste into little balls and serve it as a sweetmeat.

1 kg • 2 lb apples, pears, crab apples or quinces
300 ml • 10 fl oz • 2¼ cups medium sweet white wine
2 tablespoons honey
ground cinnamon and ginger

Cook the fruits whole, or halved if they are large, but with their skins on, with the wine and honey until they are quite pulped. 'Bray in a mortar' – or purée in a food processor or liquidiser – then sieve to remove all the bits of skin, pips etc. Return the sieved mixture to the saucepan, season it to taste with the spices and a little more sugar if the fruit was particularly tart. Continue to cook it *very* slowly, stirring now and then to prevent it sticking, till the mixture is almost solid. Cool it slightly, then roll it into little balls and serve as 'sweetmeats'.

DATE AND GINGER SWEETMEAT or LECHEMEAT

This was an immensely rich and sticky paste which could be eaten, like jams in Egypt, by itself with a spoon – although in medieval England it would be accompanied by spiced wines at the end of the meal rather than coffee and iced water as a snack. It is excellent but a little goes a long way!

100 g • 4 oz fresh dates, skinned, stoned and
chopped
150 ml • 5 fl oz • ⅔ cup sweet white wine
75 g • 3 oz stem or crystallised ginger, roughly
chopped
1 tablespoon honey
1 teaspoon ground cinnamon
50 g • 2 oz fresh brown breadcrumbs

Simmer the dates with the wine for 5 minutes. Add the ginger, honey and cinnamon and heat for a few minutes more to melt the honey and amalgamate the mixture. Turn it into a food processor and chop till it is a rough purée. Then add the breadcrumbs and process again to get them well mixed in. Remove the 'lechemeat' into a small pot and serve with individual small spoons, or roll the mixture into rather sticky sweets and serve at the end of the meal.

COMFITS

To sweeten the breath at the end of a meal it was customary to eat or suck aromatic seeds such as coriander, aniseed, fennel and carraway. These were individually, and immensely laboriously, coated in sugar, seed by seed. The process often continued over several days.

If you have the patience to make them, melt 2 tablespoons of sugar in 1 tablespoon of water. Keep the syrup warm enough to remain liquid without allowing it to caramelise. Dip each seed in the sugar, then remove it with tongs and allow it to dry thoroughly before repeating the process, again and again and again until you have built up a thick layer of sugar all over the seed. It will certainly take you all of one day and may well be spread over several if you want a really thick layer of sugar.

RENAISSANCE ITALY

Renaissance Italy with its rich and powerful city states, immensely wealthy churchmen, worldly wise popes and close links with the traditions of Imperial Rome, was a wonderful breeding ground for imaginative and extravagant cooks. Indeed, it is often forgotten that although France was to become the gastronomic mentor of Europe it was Italy that led the way.

The Italian cooks who travelled north in the wake of Catherine de Medici when she married Henri II of France took with them an interest in the scientific aspects of food, an appreciation of the regional virtues of various foodstuffs and a desire to concentrate on the specific tastes of certain foods rather than creating the gustatory mishmashes so beloved of the Middle Ages. They also understood the virtues of marinating and lengthy cooking to improve the quality of meats and fishes and had developed rudimentary recipes for puff and flaky pastries. The French enthusiastically adopted these ideas and, under the leadership of Varenne in the late seventeenth century, went on to elaborate them into the *haute cuisine* with which we are so familiar.

Late Renaissance diners were seated around long rectangular tables, decorated with ornate gold and silver centrepieces by master craftsmen such as Benvenuto Cellini. These held the salt as well as little dishes of fruits and nuts, sweetmeats and fingers of raw fennel for the guests to 'sweeten their breath' at the end of the meal.

Anything up to eight courses were served including antipasti, soups, fish dishes, meat dishes, vegetables and desserts. Each course was presented on elaborate platters laid along the table for guests to help themselves. Knifes, spoons and two pronged forks were in common usage and huge table napkins were draped over guests' elegant ruffs to protect them from the food!

Wines were drunk throughout, becoming sweeter and spicier as the meal drew to its end. Entertainment too was very much in evidence with musicians, singers, dancers and jugglers performing up the centre of the hall during breaks in the meal.

MENU

ANTIPASTO

ZUPPA DI PISELLI

BIANCO MANGIARE DI POLPA DI PESCE

OR

RISOTTO CON ANITRA SILVATICA E TARTUFI

FRICANDO

SPINACCI

TART FRESH FRUITS & NUTS
APPLES, QUINCES, PEARS

ANTIPASTO

A wide selection of small dishes of antipasti were, if anything, even more popular in the sixteenth and seventeenth centuries than they are now. The custom of laying all the dishes for every course out on the table for guests to help themselves was ideally suited to *hors d'oeuvres* which could be adapted to the season and individual tastes. In Renaissance Italy the antipasto would include sweet fruits such as melon, peaches, apricots and strawberries which were thought to aid digestion if eaten at the start of a meal. Tart fruits, apples, pears and quinces assisted the system when eaten as a finale! Any of the following dishes could be used on an antipasto table.

Sliced salami – any kind of sliced sausage *or* salami would be acceptable

Quail's eggs in their shells, *or mollé* in aspic

A dish of anchovies dressed with lemon juice

Boiled river shrimps with lemon wedges

Sogliole in carpione (see p. 106)

Fingers of fresh parmesan or peccorino cheese

Dishes of cucumber, peeled, sliced and salted

Dishes of whole radishes

Dishes of curly endive

Sliced orange salad dressed with oil and wine vinegar – aceto balsamico if possible

Plates of olives, green *or* black, but not stuffed

Salted whole almonds

Fresh apricots

Fresh peaches

Strawberries

Melon pieces

STEFANI'S ZUPPA DI PISELLI
SERVES SIX

Bartolomeo Stefani was chef to the great Gonzaga family in the second half of the seventeenth century and it is his book, *L'arte de ben cucinare*, published in 1662, which marks the end of truly Italian grand cooking. By the late seventeenth century it was the exciting new *haute cuisine* of La Varenne and the court of Versailles which had become the gastronomic 'rage' throughout aristocratic Europe.

In the original recipe whole peas, mange tout or snow peas were used; I found it more practical (and cheaper) to use good quality frozen green peas.

750 g • 1½ lb good quality frozen *or* fresh green peas

1 large onion, chopped

2–3 large cloves garlic, chopped

1.25 g • 2¼ pints • 5 cups good chicken *or* veal stock

25 g • 1 oz toasted pine nuts

15 g • ½ oz sugar

juice of 1 lemon

salt and freshly ground (if possible) white pepper

6 slices fine grain brown bread

approximately 6 tablespoons olive oil

approximately 50 g • 2 oz freshly grated parmesan

Cook the peas with the onion and garlic in the stock for 20 minutes (or in a microwave for 7 minutes) and purée them in a processor or liquidiser/blender. Meanwhile, pound the pine nuts with the sugar and lemon juice. This can be done in a pestle and mortar or in a processor or blender but the results should be reasonably coarse. Stir this mixture into the purée and season to taste with salt and pepper.

Fry the slices of bread in the olive oil till they are crisp and brown on both sides and reserve.

To serve, put a slice of fried bread in the bottom of each heated serving bowl and sprinkle it liberally with parmesan. Reheat the soup and pour it over the fried bread in each bowl. Serve with plenty more freshly grated parmesan.

SOGLIOLE IN CARPIONE★

SERVES SIX AS A STARTER
FOUR AS A MAIN COURSE

This recipe is based on the *Pesce a capucciolo* to be found in Christoforo Messisbugo's *Libro Novo* published in the late sixteenth century. Messisbugo was not in fact a cook but the *Scalco* or steward (a much grander being) to the Este family at Ferrara. As steward (and a member of

the minor nobility – he married a Ferrarese lady by the name of Agnese di Giovanni Gioccoli) he was responsible for the actual presentation of the meals, as well as overseeing their preparation. His *sogliole* or *pesce* would have been served as part of the huge antipasto course but is quite substantial enough to make a fish dish on its own.

750 g • 1½ lb sole, filletted and each fillet cut in
half lengthways
25 g • 1 oz wholemeal flour
salt and freshly ground black pepper
5 generous tablespoons olive oil

1 medium onion, very finely sliced
2 large cloves garlic, very finely chopped or
crushed
1 stick celery, very finely sliced
¼ of a bulb of fennel, very finely sliced
1 carrot, scrubbed and very finely sliced
6 tablespoons dry white wine
juice of 2 lemons
1 level teaspoon cinnamon
3 bay leaves
4 cloves
25 g • 1 oz toasted pine nuts
25 g • 1 oz sultanas

Coat the fillets of fish in the seasoned flour then fry them gently in the oil for 3–5 minutes, depending on size or till they are cooked and lightly browned. Remove them and drain them on some kitchen paper towel. Gently cook the vegetables in the same oil till they are soft and lightly coloured. Add the wine, lemon juice and cinnamon and cook briskly for a couple of minutes till they have reduced slightly.

Lay the bay leaves over the fish fillets then sprinkle on the cloves, pine nuts and sultanas. Spoon over the vegetables with their juice, cover the dish and leave it in a cool larder or a refrigerator for a minimum of 24, preferably 48, hours. Remove from the fridge for at least an hour before serving with lots of crusty fresh bread.

BIANCO MANGIARE DI POLPA DI PESCE
SERVES SIX

Blanc-manger's, *bianco mangiare's* or 'white things to eat', popular throughout the middle ages, still appeared at every Renaissance banquet. Filled with highly prized, delicately flavoured almonds and spices, they provided an excellent background for the artist/cook to indulge himself with ornate decorations. The *bianco mangiare* could be made with white meats or fishes and would have been heavily sprinkled with sugar. If you find this too much of a gastronomic shock, just leave it out.

350 g • 12 oz of any firm fleshed white fish

a little white wine and ½ a lemon, sliced

75 g • 3 oz rinsed white rice

50 g • 2 oz ground almonds

210 ml • 7 fl oz • ⅞ cup (whole) milk

salt and white pepper

1 tablespoon sugar *optional*

TO DECORATE

little cooked rice coloured with saffron or turmeric, some finely chopped parsley, sliced pistachio nuts, toasted pine nuts *or* anything else colourful with which to decorate the

bianco mangiare

Cook the fish, with the sliced lemon, in just enough white wine and water to cover it. Drain it, reserving the cooking liquid, remove any bones and skin and pound it to a paste in a pestle and mortar or a food processor. Boil the rice in the reserved fish liquid (with a little extra water if there is not enough) till it is cooked but not mushy; drain it. Mix the ground almonds to a paste with the milk then add the rice and the fish. If the mixture is too 'sloppy' cook it gently over a low heat for a few minutes to reduce the liquid. Season with salt and white pepper. You can also add the sugar at this stage although in the seventeenth century it would have been sprinkled over the dish rather than mixed into it. Spoon the mixture into a ring mould or soufflé dish and chill for a couple of hours.

To serve the *bianco mangiare*, turn it out onto a dish, sprinkle it with the sugar and decorate it as the spirit moves you. If it is in a ring it will look very attractive with the centre filled with watercress or a mixture of green herbs and salad; if it is in a mould you can use nuts, herbs and spices to make as complex and elaborate a pattern as you wish.

RISOTTO CON ANITRA SILVATICA E TARTUFI
or RISOTTO WITH WILD DUCK *or* ANY GAME BIRD & TRUFFLES *or* MUSHROOMS
SERVES SIX

A risotto served with wild duck was a favourite dish at the court of Mantua but the visit of Pope Paul III and the Duke of Ferrara in 1543 inspired the Mantuan chief cook to splash out and cover his risotto with thinly sliced truffles. Alas, the price of truffles is so astronomical that only the visit of a pope could justify the expense involved in using them today. If wild duck is not available, pigeons or any other small, dark game bird will serve equally well.

2 wild duck *or* 3–4 wood pigeons *or* other small
game birds, cleaned
75 g • 3 oz butter
3 medium onions, 2 chopped fairly small,
1 chopped very finely

10 cloves of garlic, 8 halved, 2 chopped very
finely

300 ml • 10 fl oz • 1¼ cups good quality dry
Italian white wine

a generous grind of pepper and ½ teaspoon salt

8 cloves

25 g • 1 oz *porcini or* other dried mushrooms,
soaked in 120 ml • 4 fl oz • ½ cup warm water

500 g • 18 oz Italian rice

1 litre • 1¾ pints • 4¼ cups chicken *or* veal stock

50–75 g • 2–3 oz finely sliced truffles *or* button
mushrooms wiped, sliced very finely and tossed
in a little lemon juice

Melt 50 g • 2 oz of the butter in a heavy casserole
and gently fry the 2 roughly chopped onions and
the 8 halved garlic cloves till they are lightly
coloured. Turn the heat up, add the birds and fry
briskly till the birds are well coloured on all sides.
Throw on the wine, reduce the heat and add the
salt, pepper, cloves and soaked *porcini*. Bring to
the simmer, cover and cook very gently for 2
hours or till the meat is falling off the bone.

Remove the birds, cool slightly and bone them
(the bones can be kept to make stock); cut the
meat into bite size pieces. Remove the garlic
halves and cloves and discard them. Skim the
excess fat (if there is any) from the juices and
return the meat to them.

Meanwhile, heat the remaining butter in a wide
pan and gently cook the remaining finely chopped onion and garlic till it is softened and golden.
Add the rice, cook for a minute or two, then add
the stock. Bring to the boil and simmer gently for
approximately 15 minutes or till the liquid is all
absorbed. Season to taste with salt and white
pepper.

To serve, arrange the rice in a ring around a
serving dish, smoothing off the top. Cover the
ring of rice with the sliced truffles or mushrooms.
Pile the meat with its juices into the middle of the
ring and serve at once followed by a good salad.

FRICANDÒ *or* BRAISED BEEF *or* VEAL WITH HAM AND CARROTS★

SERVES SIX

It is said that this dish travelled with Catherine de Medici from Florence to France when she married Henri II in the mid 1500s, then back to Italy 250 years later with the Napoleonic invasion. It can be made with veal or beef and larded with ham or *prosciutto* – depending on the depths of your pocket.

1 kg • 2 lb loin of veal *or* topside of beef
3 thin (but not very thin) slices of ham *or* Parma ham/prosciutto
5 carrots, scrubbed
50 g • 2 oz butter
4 sticks of celery, chopped small
2 small onions, peeled and finely chopped
300 ml • 10 fl oz • 1¼ cups Marsala
150 ml • 5 fl oz • ⅔ cup veal, beef or chicken stock
salt and pepper

Cut the meat lengthways in three places almost to the bottom of the joint. Lay one slice of ham or prosciutto in each cut. Slice one of the carrots very thinly lengthways and lay that inside the ham. Tie the meat back into a roll shape.

Melt the butter in a heavy casserole. Add the onions, celery and remaining carrots, diced small with the meat and fry them all briskly till they are lightly browned all over. Add the Marsala and the stock, bring to the boil, cover the pan and simmer very gently for 2 hours. Remove the meat from the pan and purée the juices with the vegetables. Return the purée to the pan and season to taste with salt and pepper. To serve, reheat the meat in the sauce, then slice it thickly, lay it on a platter and spoon the sauce over the top. Serve it with lightly cooked leaf spinach.

FRIED POLENTA *or* BUCKWHEAT CAKES
SERVES SIX

Although the cornmeal which is used for the *polenta* dishes of northern Italy today arrived in Europe in the mid-sixteenth century it did not really catch on till over a hundred years later. Not that mealy type dishes, both boiled and fried,

were not popular with Renaissance cooks; they merely used wheat rather than corn meal. Fried buckwheat cakes or matchsticks are excellent as a vegetable or can be served with a soft cheese such as a mild gorgonzola as a dish in their own right.

225 g • 8 oz buckwheat

950 ml • 32 fl oz • 4 cups water

plenty of salt and freshly ground black pepper

2 tablespoons wholemeal *or* wholewheat flour

approximately 6 tablespoons olive oil

225–350 g • 8–12 oz gorgonzola *or* other soft Italian cheese *optional*

Put the buckwheat in a large pan with the water, salt and pepper, bring to the boil and simmer for approximately 20 minutes or till the water is nearly all absorbed and the buckwheat soft. Add the flour, stir well into the mixture and season further if necessary. Spoon the mixture onto a floured board, shape into a thin rectangle approximately 1 cm • ½ inch thick and leave to cool. To cook, cut the buckwheat cake into thinnish matchsticks. Heat the oil in a shallow pan and fry the matchsticks briskly on all sides till they are well tanned. Drain on kitchen paper towel and keep warm till they are ready to be served. Serve alone as a vegetable or accompanied by fingers of the cheese as a starter or light main course.

SPINACH 'FRIED' WITH VINEGAR

SERVES FOUR TO SIX

The *Opera* of Bartolomeo Scappi, published in 1570, was one of the most important cookery works to come out of the Renaissance. As cook to some of the grandest cardinals of his time Scappi had ample opportunity to experiment with the new techniques of braising and 'casserole' cooking, pastas, pastries and the serving of vegetables such as spinach as complete dishes rather than elements in a stew or soup.

1.5 kg • 3 lb fresh spinach, washed, most of the water shaken off it and roughly chopped

75 g • 3 oz butter

4 tablespoons wine vinegar

salt and freshly ground black pepper

Melt the butter in a large pan and add the spinach. Cook briskly for a few minutes, stirring well so that all the spinach gets well coated with butter. Add the vinegar, turn the heat down, cover the pan and simmer for 7–10 minutes or till the spinach is quite cooked. Season to taste with salt and freshly ground black pepper and serve.

PASTA

Various shapes and sizes of pasta had been used in Italy from the middle ages onwards although they were treated as something of a luxury dish. Two of the most popular types were lasagne and vermicelli but flat noodles and macaroni were also being made by the middle of the seventeenth century. The pasta shapes were cooked in meat or

fish stocks although it is not clear whether they were drained or served in their liquid. Cheese was normally sprinkled over the pasta although medieval Arabic additions of sugar and cinnamon were also popular.

Use any pasta shape that you fancy, fresh or dried and allow 75–100 g • 3–4 oz of pasta per head. Cook it in fast boiling, well-salted water or stock for 3–4 minutes if it is fresh, 10–12 minutes if it is dried, but in either case only as long as the pasta remains *al dente* or slightly chewy. If you have cooked it in water, drain it to serve; if you have used stock drain it or not as you feel inclined and serve it with plenty of freshly grated parmesan (25–50 g • 1–2 oz per head), freshly ground black pepper and, if you wish to be genuinely seventeenth century about it, a generous sprinkling of sugar and of ground cinnamon.

FRITTOLE
MAKES APPROXIMATELY THIRTY FRITTOLE

Every country in Europe has its own way of deep frying batters to make sweet or savoury 'nibbles'. 'Frittole' have been served in Venice since the sixteenth century and Venetians claim that 'frittole are like women – if they are not round and a little fat, they are no good . . .'

25 g • 1 oz sultanas
2 tablespoons sweet white wine *or* liqueur
20 g • 1½ fresh yeast
1 teaspoon sugar
100 g • 4 oz each plain wholemeal and white flour
generous pinch of salt
grated rind of 1 lemon
1 teaspoon cinnamon
clean oil for deep frying
sugar *optional*

Soak the raisins in the liqueur for at least ½ an hour. Dissolve the yeast with the sugar in 2 tablespoons warm water and leave it in a warm place until it froths. Mix the flour with the salt, lemon rind and cinnamon. Add the yeast and mix to a soft dough with more water. Mix in the soaked raisins and any remaining liqueur. Put the dough in a bowl in a warm place, covered with a cloth, to rise – it should take about half an hour and almost double its size.

Heat the oil and drop the batter into it in generous teaspoonfuls; the frittole should take a couple of minutes each to cook. Drain them on kitchen paper. Traditionally they are served well drenched with sugar but I prefer them as they are. If you cannot serve them immediately they will reheat quite successfully, uncovered, in a moderate oven for approximately 10 minutes.

CERTOSINO *or* PAN SPEZIALE★

The original of this scrumptiously rich, traditional Bolognese Christmas cake was finally written down by the monks of the Abbey of Certosa at the behest of the Cardinal Lambertini who left Bologna to become Pope Benedetto XIV in 1740. Ideally it should be allowed to mature for several days, weeks, or even months before it is eaten.

75 g • 3 oz raisins

2 tablespoons of rum *or* brandy

225 g • 8 oz honey

40 g • 1½ oz butter

1 teaspoon cinnamon

1 teaspoon whole aniseeds *optional*

300 g • 10 oz plain wholemeal flour

150 g • 6 oz cooked sieved apple, preferably cooking apple

150 g • 6 oz roughly chopped mixed almonds and walnuts *or* pecans – in whatever proportion you like

40 g • 1½ pine nuts

150 g • 6 oz mixed candied orange and lemon peel and crystallised ginger in whatever proportions you like

50 g • 2 oz bitter chocolate broken into reasonably small pieces

1½ teaspoons bicarbonate of soda

apricot jam and extra candied fruit and nuts to decorate

Steep the raisins in the rum or brandy for at least half an hour. Meanwhile, gently warm the honey with the butter and 3 tablespoons of water till it is melted but do not allow it to boil. Sift the flour with the spices into a large bowl. Mix in the honey and butter, then add the apple, nuts, peel, chocolate, raisins and brandy or rum, mixing them thoroughly. Dissolve the bicarbonate of soda in a tablespoon of warm water and mix it into the dough. Turn it into a 20–23 cm • 8–9 inch cake tin, greased and lined or with a loose bottom and bake in a slow oven (140°C • 275°F • Gas Mark 1) for 2 hours or till the cake is slightly risen, firm and cooked through. Remove from the tin and cool on a rack. The cake can be stored wrapped in foil or in a freezer. When you are ready to use it, brush the top with apricot jam and decorate with candied fruits and/or nuts.

GEORGIAN
ENGLAND

Life in eighteenth-century England was a busy, bustling affair especially in the cities with their taverns, gin shops and 'confectioners' for the better class of society, their political satirists, broadsheets and meetings, their open markets, theatres and entertainers – and, of course, the dandies, 'macaronis' and other fashionable members of 'society'; and eating formed an important part of this bustle, whether it was done at home or abroad.

Large families, when you include the servants, were still normal so it was important for the mistress of even a small house to know how to organise her ménage. By the mid-eighteenth century most middle class ladies could read, or at least read enough to follow the directions in the many manuals and 'directories' published for their use. These were often written by retired cooks and housekeepers, both men and women, dedicated 'to the Honourable . . . for whom the author lately served as housekeeper'. Other professionals in the food business also got into print: William Verral was the landlord of the White Hart Inn at Lewes in Sussex; Elizabeth Raffald ran a catering business and started the first domestic agency in Manchester – inbetween producing thirteen daughters . . . Richard Bradley was Professor of Botany at the University of Cambridge but had a keen amateur interest in collecting recipes. But whoever compiled them, all include directions not only for cooking but for preserving and distilling, very important parts of a housekeeper's job before the arrival of mass produced foods; marketing, planning menus and the arranging and laying out of tables.

Service à la Russe, or the serving of meals in courses of individual dishes, did not really become popular till Victorian times. In the eighteenth century it was still the custom to divide the meal into two, or occasionally three, courses of

MENU

A 'Soup for Supper'

A 'Fasting Day Soup'

Eggs au Miroir

Stewed Soles from Yarmouth

Salmon Pye

Bombarded Veal

Potatoe Pudding

Stewed Cucumber

'Spinage' with Cream

Quakin' Pudding

Peach Fritters & Syllabubs

mixed sweet and savoury dishes. The first course normally contained soups and a preponderance of 'made' savoury dishes, the second the roasts and desserts. Exactly how these were arranged on the table was of the utmost importance and every cookery book contains at least one sample 'plan' of how the dishes should be laid out: so that the table should be 'well covered without being crowded'. You will also find notes attached to recipes – 'This is a good dish for a corner' – referring to its place on the table. This system did not make for an easy life for your guests – it could be quite a problem if the dish that you wanted was large and at the other end of the table and there was no servant around – but it did look pretty!

To serve an eighteenth-century meal correctly today one would need to be entertaining a fairly large number of people so as to use all the dishes. If you wish to serve only a small group, pick the dishes you fancy and serve them in courses as with a normal twentieth-century meal. Cheese was sometimes served at the end of the meal to 'close the stomach'. A wide range of wines were available to eighteenth-century diners so feel free to chose whatever you think would suit the meal best.

WILLIAM VERRAL'S SOUP FOR SUPPER

SERVES SIX

The introduction to Verral's recipe runs as follows: 'This may seem to be but a simple thing to place amongst these high matters; but I never see it come from table without a terrible wound in it. If it has but the approbation of few it will pay very well for the room it takes up here.' Simple, but very rich . . . I find it is best served well chilled when its sweet richness becomes a virtue rather than a fault.

900 ml • 1½ pints • 3¾ cups whole milk

200 ml • 7 fl oz • ⅞ cup double *or* heavy cream

peeled rind and juice of 1 lemon

15 coriander seeds

3 bay leaves

½ stick *or* ½ teaspoonful of ground cinnamon

1 teaspoon sugar

100 g • 4 oz ground almonds

3 egg yolks

juice of 1 large orange

salt and white pepper

Put the milk and cream in a pan with the lemon rind, coriander seeds, bay leaves, cinnamon and sugar. Bring slowly to the boil, simmer for a few minutes then allow to cool. Add the ground almonds, bring slowly back to the boil, again simmer for a few minutes then rub the mixture through a sieve. Mix the egg yolks with the orange and lemon juices and whisk them into the soup. Again heat slowly but do not boil. Season lightly with salt and pepper. Cool and then chill thoroughly before serving with hot white or milk rolls.

ELIZA SMITH'S FASTING DAY SOUP
SERVES SIX

Even in the late eighteenth century 'fast' or non-meat eating days were still observed in the Church of England so it was important to have a range of dishes which could be made tasty without the use of meat or meat stock.

75 g • 3 oz *each* fresh spinach and fresh sorrel *or*,
if the sorrel is not available, 150 g • 6 oz fresh
spinach, washed and roughly chopped
a handful of parsley, washed and
roughly chopped
½ small lettuce, chopped
25 g • 1 oz butter
1 medium onion stuck with approximately
15 cloves
40 g • 1½ oz fresh brown breadcrumbs
1.5 litres • 2½ pints • 6¼ cups water
salt and pepper
3 egg yolks

90 ml • 3 fl oz • ⅓ cup white wine
juice of 1 lemon
40 g • 1½ oz pistachio nuts,
chopped fairly finely

Melt the butter in large pan and lightly cook the spinach, sorrel, parsley and lettuce for 5 minutes or till it is well wilted. Add the onion stuck with the cloves, breadcrumbs, water and some salt and pepper. Bring to the boil and simmer for 20 minutes. Remove the onion, purée the soup in a liquidiser or processor then strain it through a coarse sieve. Return it to the pan. Whisk the egg yolks with the wine, lemon and nuts and whisk them into the soup. Cook it gently for a few minutes, but do not boil. Adjust the seasoning to taste and serve.

EGGS AU MIROIR
SERVES SIX

This recipe comes also from William Verral's *Complete System of Cookery* first published in 1759. Verral was the landlord of the White Hart Inn at Lewes in Sussex and had learnt his cookery under 'the celebrated Mr de St Clouet, sometime since COOK to his Grace the Duke of Newcastle'. Following his master, Verral was a great believer in the copious use of vegetables as a base to his

stocks and sauces, in contrast to the majority of his contemporaries who regarded immensely concentrated meat stocks as the only starting point for further elaboration. Verral was also a liberal user of cream but since its richness was always tempered by orange or lemon juice, or both, the result is a freshness in his flavours which never cloys.

25 g • 1 oz butter
10–12 spring onions *or* scallions, finely chopped
3 handfuls of parsley, finely chopped
6 large eggs (if you want to use this as a luncheon dish you can use 2 eggs per person and increase all the other ingredients by one third)
300 ml • 10 fl oz • 1¼ cups double *or* heavy cream
juice of 3 small oranges and 2 small lemons
salt and white pepper

Rub the bottom of a flan dish large enough to hold the eggs with the butter and spread the onions and parsley over it. Carefully break the eggs into the dish. Mix the cream with the juices, season them fairly generously and pour them over the eggs. Bake in a moderately cool oven (160°C • 325°F • Gas Mark 3) for 15 minutes or till the whites of the eggs are just set. The eggs can be served warm or cold with brown toast or fresh brown bread, and a green salad if you want to make it a more substantial dish.

A SALOMONGUNDY

A very popular eighteenth-century dish, a salo-mongundy was a sort of *hors d'oeuvre* made up of contrasting sharp and bland flavoured ingredients arranged on a large dish or in little dishes displayed as the centrepiece of a table. It was also an excellent way of 'using up' remains. Every eighteenth-century recipe book has at least three recipes for salomongundy, so, as long as you get a good contrast of flavours, you can include almost anything; I am listing suggestions below. Decorate the gaps between the foods on your platter or between the dishes with fresh herbs and flowers and the whole thing will look quite spectacular.

BLAND FOODS

hard boiled eggs, yolks and whites separated
cooked chicken meat (very popular) *or* slithers of cooked veal, pork, duck or pigeon
cooked white fishes *or* cooked herring
lettuces, chopped *or* sliced fine – Romaine for preference
chopped celery and cucumbers
artichoke hearts and raw mushrooms
soft cheeses
boiled onions, either small and whole *or* large and sliced

SHARP FOODS

anchovies (essential in all salomongundies)
any kind of pickle that you have available
diced fresh *or* pickled lemon
sharp oil and vinegar dressing

ELIZA SMITH'S SALMON PYE
SERVES SIX

Eliza Smith died around 1732 but her book, *The Compleat Housewife or Accomplished Gentlewoman's Companion* went through eighteen editions and was the first English cookery book to be published in America. As did most eighteenth-century cookery books, it contained cures and remedies, menus for different times of the year and 'directions for marketing' along with over six hundred excellent recipes. Her salmon pie could be made with tinned salmon but is much better with fresh.

750 g • 1½ lb fresh salmon – a tail piece will do very well

1 lemon, sliced

450 ml • 15 fl oz • 2 cups *each* water and white wine

salt, pepper and a bunch of fresh herbs *or* a *bouquet garni* if fresh are not available

325 g • 6 oz *each* plain white and wholemeal *or* wholewheat flour

60 g • 2½ oz *each* butter and lard

3 hard boiled egg yolks

9 anchovies, chopped finely and 1 tablespoon of oil from the tin

100 g • 4 oz cooked mussels, cockles *or* oysters, chopped finely – frozen will do very well

50 g • 2 oz fresh brown breadcrumbs

50 g • 2 oz very soft butter

salt, pepper and a pinch of nutmeg

a handful of chopped fresh herbs (parsley, thyme, sage, rosemary, chervil) *or* 2 teaspoons dried mixed herbs

1 egg *optional*

Put the salmon in a pan with the lemon slices, water and wine, seasoning and herbs. Bring it to the boil and simmer for approximately 15 minutes or till the salmon is cooked; this could also be done in a microwave. Remove the salmon, reserving the cooking juices, skin and bone it.

Meanwhile, make the pastry by rubbing the fats into the mixed flours then adding enough cold water to make a stiff dough. Chill it if necessary then roll out two thirds and line a loose

bottomed 23 cm • 9 inch cake tin. If you do not have a loose bottomed or sided tin you might be wise to line it with foil under the pastry. Set aside.

Mash the hard boiled egg yolks and mix with the anchovies, mussels or oysters, breadcrumbs, soft butter, anchovy oil, herbs and seasoning; form the mixture into small balls. Break up the salmon and fill the pie with the salmon pieces interspersed with the 'forcemeat' balls. Top the pie with the remaining pastry, leaving a hole to pour in some juices, and brush it with the beaten egg if you want a shiny top. Bake it in a moderately hot oven (190°C • 375°F • Gas Mark 5) for 30–35 minutes or till the pastry is cooked and golden.

Strain and reheat the cooking juices. Pour 120–180 ml • 4–6 fl oz • ½–¾ cup of them through the hold in the pastry lid. Serve the pie warm or cold, with a green vegetable or salad.

MRS RAFFALD'S BOILED MACKAREL
SERVES SIX

This recipe comes from Elizabeth Raffald's immensely popular *Experienced English Housekeeper, for the USE and EASE of Ladies, Housekeepers, Cooks &c.* which was to be found amongst the wedding gifts of almost any young lady who walked up the aisle in the latter half of the eighteenth century! The sauce is rumbustuous but well suited to the strong flavour of mackerel.

6 small *or* 3 large mackerel, cleaned

2 tablespoons white wine vinegar

4 anchovies

juice of 2 lemons

1 tablespoon of walnut *or* mushroom ketchup *or*,
if neither is available, Worcester sauce

½ teaspoon mace

1 teaspoon *each* of soft butter and flour

1 teaspoon horseradish sauce

salt and pepper

Put the mackerel in a pan just big enough to hold them, add the vinegar and cover them with water. Bring them to the boil and simmer them gently for 10–15 minutes depending on size. Meanwhile chop the anchovies and put them, with the lemon juice, ketchup and mace, in a medium pan. When the fish are cooked, remove them and set them aside. Add 600 ml • 1 pint • 2½ cups of the cooking water to the other ingredients, bring them to the boil and simmer them gently for 5 minutes. Bone and fillet the fish, lay them in a serving dish, cover them and keep them warm. Mix the softened butter and flour with the horseradish, add a little of the sauce to it then return the lot to the saucepan. Continue to cook for a couple of minutes till the sauce has thickened slightly. Adjust the seasoning, if it needs it, and spoon over the fish. Decorate with fresh herbs before serving with a bland vegetable such as steamed potatoes or rice.

RICHARD BRADLEY'S STEWED SOLE FROM YARMOUTH
SERVES SIX

Richard Bradley's *Country Housewife and Lady's Director*, first published in 1727 and on its sixth edition by 1736, was filled with useful advice and recipes collected from the most diverse of sources. Surprisingly the sauce, which combines several quite vigorous flavours, does not over-power the fish.

6 sole (lemon rather than Dover), filletted
240 ml • 8 fl oz • 1 cup *each* good quality beef
consommé, water and light red wine
rind of 1 lemon
3 anchovies, chopped *or*
2 teaspoons anchovy essence
1 medium onion, chopped finely
15 g • ½ oz butter
2 bouquet garni
salt, pepper and a pinch each of ground cloves,
mace and nutmeg
25 g • 1 oz each soft butter and flour

Prepare the fish and set the fillets aside. Put all the other ingredients except the softened butter and flour in a large flat pan, bring them to the boil and simmer them for 5–10 minutes. Add the fish fillets and cook at a gentle simmer for 5–7 minutes or till the fish is cooked. This dish would do well in a microwave where it should not take more than 3–4 minutes on high. Remove the fillets to a warmed serving dish. Strain the cooking juices and return them to the pan. Mash the flour and butter together and add it gradually to the sauce. Reheat but do not allow to boil. Pour over the fish fillets and decorate with some watercress or fresh herbs before serving.

MRS RAFFALD'S 'BOMBARDED' VEAL OR PORK
SERVES EIGHT TO TEN

This dish is not worth making except in a fairly large piece so as to allow room for the various stuffings. It is excellent with veal but if the expense is daunting it works just as well with pork. For reasons of expense I have also replaced the oysters in the original with cockles or mussels.

approximately 1.5 kg • 3 lb loin of veal *or* pork
in one piece *or* 4 fillets of veal *or* pork, flattened

STUFFING ONE

50 g • 2 oz brown breadcrumbs
50 g • 2 oz fat bacon, chopped small
2 anchovies, chopped small
grated rind ½ lemon
a pinch of cayenne pepper
2 sprigs of fresh marjoram *or* 1 teaspoon of dried
a generous handful of chopped parsley
1 small egg
30 ml • 1 fl oz • ⅛ cup double *or* heavy cream
salt and pepper and ground nutmeg

STUFFING TWO

450 g • 1 lb fresh or 225 g • 8 oz frozen spinach,
chopped, lightly cooked and very well drained
salt, pepper and nutmeg

STUFFING THREE

100 g • 4 oz cockles *or* mussels, fresh cooked *or*
frozen – if you use mussels they should be

chopped roughly
25 g • 1 oz brown breadcrumbs
1 small egg
salt and pepper

2 onions and 2 carrots

SAUCE

40 g • 1½ oz butter *or* low fat margarine
75 g • 3 oz button mushrooms, sliced
20 g • ¾ oz flour
6 cooked artichoke hearts, drained and quartered
– frozen or tinned will do
juice of 1–2 lemons *or* 1–2 teaspoons lemon
pickle
1–2 teaspoons mushroom ketchup
salt and pepper

Mix the ingredients for the first stuffing well
together and season generously; set aside. Season
the spinach for the second stuffing generously.
Mix and season the ingredients for the third
stuffing. Make three deep, lengthways cuts in the
loin of veal and fill each with a different stuffing

evenly spread along its length. If you are using fillets lay them on top of each other lengthways with the stuffings evenly spread between them. Tie the meat neatly to prevent the stuffings escaping, or wrap it in a caul, then put in a deep pot with the onion and carrot and just cover with water. Bring slowly to the boil, skimming any skum which may rise to the surface, cover and simmer gently for 2–2½ hours, depending on

the weight of the joint. Remove the meat and keep it warm.

To make the sauce, melt the butter in a pan and lightly fry the mushrooms for a couple of minutes. Add the flour, stir around for two minutes then gradually add 450 ml • 15 fl oz • 2 cups of the cooking juices taken from the bottom of the pot thus avoiding any fat. This can be done with a bulb baster which sucks the stock from below the fat or by pouring the juices into a jug separator which allows you to pour the juices from the bottom of the jug. Cook the sauce gently till it thickens slightly, add the artichokes and continue to cook till they are warmed through. Season the sauce with the lemon juice or pickle and the mushroom ketchup; you can also add extra salt and pepper but I do not find it necessary.

Remove the meat from its caul or strings, carve it across the stuffings and serve accompanied by the warmed sauce and plain vegetables which will not mask the sauce.

STEW'D BEEF STEAKS
FROM THE SPRING GARDENS AT VAUXHALL
SERVES SIX

Like the recipe for 'stew'd sole' on p. 126, this recipe comes from Richard Bradley's *Lady's Director*. Vauxhall Gardens were the most popular of eighteenth-century London's 'amusement parks' where both rich and poor could listen to music, dine, dance and watch the world go by. According to Mr Bradley, their 'stew'd beefsteaks' were 'very much approved'.

6 thinnish slices of steak suitable for frying – it is
unnecessary to use fillet, rump or sirloin steak
but you will need something of better quality
than mere stewing steak
2 slices of fat bacon, chopped small
2 onions, chopped finely
peel of 1 lemon
5 cloves
3 anchovy fillets
a generous bunch of fresh herbs (parsley, thyme,
bayleaf, sage) *or* 3 *bouquet garni*
3 tablespoons red *or* white wine vinegar
300 ml • 10 fl oz • 1¼ cups dryish white wine
150 ml • 5 fl oz • ⅔ cup water
salt and pepper
25 g • 1 oz butter
25 g • 1 oz flour

Put the steaks in a heavy bottomed pan or an
ovenproof casserole and add all the ingredients
except the butter and flour. Bring them slowly to
the boil, cover and simmer gently on the hob or
in a moderate oven for 20–30 minutes or till the
meat is cooked and tender. Remove the steaks
from the cooking juices and dry them on some
kitchen paper towel. Strain the cooking juices
and discard the 'bits'. Toss the steaks in the flour.
Melt the butter in the pan and lightly fry the
floured steaks till they are tanned and slightly
crisp on both sides. Remove them to a heated
serving dish. Add the rest of the flour to the
butter, cook for a couple of minutes, then gradually add the strained cooking juices. Stir and
simmer for a couple of minutes till you are sure
the flour is well cooked and the sauce slightly
thickened. Adjust the seasoning to taste, pour
over the steaks, garnish with a little watercress or
parsley and serve at once with a simple vegetable
such as steamed potatoes so as not to drown the
sauce.

POTATOE – PUDDING, BAKED

FROM MR SHEPHERD OF WINDMILL STREET
SERVES SIX

Mr Bradley certainly had the knack of choosing his sources; this is yet another good recipe from his *Director*. If you wanted to make a more substantial dish of it, a few ounces of cheese mixed in would turn it into a very pleasant luncheon dish.

1.5 kg • 3 lb potatoes, scrubbed

2 large carrots, finely grated

juice of 2 oranges

50 g • 2 oz butter

2 eggs

1 tablespoon orange flower water *optional*

1 teaspoon sugar

salt and pepper

Steam or microwave the potatoes and peel them or not, depending on whether you like skins in your mashed potato. Purée them with a masher or through a ricer (but not in a food processor) then add all the other ingredients and beat them thoroughly into the potato. Adjust the seasoning to taste. Spoon into a dish and bake in a moderate oven (180°C • 350°F • Gas Mark 4) for 20 minutes or till the top is lightly browned. Serve at once.

RICHARD BRADLEY'S STEWED CUCUMBERS

FROM THE DEVIL TAVERN, FLEET STREET
SERVES SIX

You seldom see cucumbers served other than raw these days although they cook surprisingly well, retaining their crunch when you would expect them to go flabby. Eighteenth-century recipe books abound with recipes for 'stew'd cucumber', 'farced' cucumber and baked cucumber, all excellent.

2 large cucumbers, sliced thickly but not peeled

4 medium onions, chopped finely

300 ml • 10 fl oz • 1¼ cups light red wine

2 tablespoons well seasoned flour

50 g • 2 oz butter

180 ml • 6 fl oz • ¾ cup water

Put the cucumbers with the onion and 60 ml • 2 fl oz • ¼ cup of the wine into a pan, cover them and cook them gently for 10 minutes, stirring now and then. Remove them from the heat and drain them; dry them on kitchen paper towel and toss in the seasoned flour. Meanwhile, melt the butter in a large pan. Fry the cucumber and onions briskly for several minutes till they are beginning to colour. Slowly add the rest of the wine and the water, stirring all the time to remove any burnt bits off the bottom of the pan. Bring back to the boil and simmer for a couple of minutes to cook the sauce. Adjust the seasoning to taste and serve at once.

WILLIAM VERRAL'S FRENCH BEANS WITH A WHITE SAUCE
SERVES SIX

The orange juice in Verral's recipe makes the sauce golden rather than white, but none the less delicious.

750 g • 1½ lb French green beans *or*
haricots verts, topped, tailed and
thinly sliced if necessary

12 spring onions *or* scallions, finely chopped

180 fl oz • 6 fl oz • ¾ cup chicken stock

2 egg yolks

juice of 2 oranges

salt and pepper

Steam or cook the beans till they are just done but still slightly crunchy; drain and keep warm. Simmer the spring onions in the chicken stock for 3–4 minutes or till the onions are softening slightly. Mix the egg yolks with the orange juice and whisk it into the onions and stock. Season to taste and pour over the beans just before serving.

WILLIAM VERRAL'S 'SPINAGE' WITH CREAM & EGGS *or* FRY'D BREAD
SERVES SIX

'This', says Mr Verral, 'being a pretty genteel dish, it is a pity to leave it out.' I can only agree . . . Serve it with fried bread as a vegetable, with eggs if you wish to turn it into a lunch or supper dish.

1.5 kg • 3 lb fresh spinach, washed and well dried

50 g • 2 oz butter

salt and pepper

2 onions, peeled and halved

1 teaspoon ground nutmeg

30 ml • 10 fl oz • 1¼ cups double *or* heavy cream

juice of 2 oranges

3 slices toasted *or* fried wholemeal *or* wholewheat bread *or* 6 eggs

Put the spinach in a pan with the butter, salt and pepper, cover it and cook it for 5–10 minutes or till it is well wilted. Drain it very thoroughly then return it to the pan with the onions, nutmeg and cream. Bring it back to the simmer and cook for 5 minutes. Remove the onions and add the orange juice. Adjust the seasoning to taste and serve surrounded with triangles of toasted or fried bread.

If you wish to cook it with the eggs, turn the finished spinach into an ovenproof dish and make six hollows into which break the six eggs. Bake them in a moderate oven (180°C • 350°F • Gas Mark 4) for 15 minutes or till the eggs are set; serve at once.

WILLIAM VERRAL'S PEACH FRITTERS WITH RHENISH WINE
SERVES SIX

Although Verral calls this dish 'a fritter' he mentions neither batter nor flour. Nor does he specify the quantity of lard to be used for frying. I suspect that he intended the peaches to be deep fried but I find that shallow frying in butter or low fat margarine is a lot quicker and cleaner and still tastes excellent.

6 large peaches *or*
9 small ones, halved *or*
quartered, but not skinned, with the stones
removed but reserved
1½–2 tablespoons sugar, depending on the
ripeness of the peaches
2 sticks *or* 1 teaspoon ground cinnamon
peel of 3 lemons
approximately 600 ml • 20 fl oz • 2½ cups
'Rhenish' or medium sweet white wine
butter *or* low fat margarine for frying

Put the peaches in a bowl with the sugar, cinnamon, lemon peel and enough wine just to cover them. Leave to marinate for 4–24 hours. Remove the peaches and dry them on kitchen paper towel. Put the marinade in a pan with the peach kernels, cracked if possible, and 150 ml • 5 fl oz • ⅔ cup of water, bring to the boil and simmer for 5 minutes. Melt the butter or low fat margarine in a flattish pan and lightly fry the dried peach pieces until they are heated through and lightly browned on all sides. Strain the sauce and serve it at once with the peaches. You can also serve cream but I feel it masks the flavour of the sauce.

MRS RAFFALD'S CHOCOLATE PUFFS
MAKES APPROXIMATELY TWENTY

These meringue-like little biscuits make an excellent alternative to after-dinner mints or *petits fours*.

1 large egg white
100 g • 4 oz sugar
25 g • 1 oz good quality dark chocolate, finely grated

Beat the egg white till very stiff. Then beat in the sugar and grated chocolate; the mixture will go rather runny in the process but it does not matter. Grease a sheet of foil and drop *very small* teaspoonfuls of the mixture onto it allowing a certain amount of room for each puff to spread. Bake the puffs in a cool oven (110°C • 225°F • Gas Mark ¼) for an hour or till they are completely dried out. Gently prise them off the foil and store in an airtight box ready for use.

A QUAKIN' PUDDING
SERVES SIX

Eighteenth-century 'quaking puddings' had a very high proportion of cream and eggs, making them both excessively rich and very wobbly when turned out – hence the name. I find that a greater proportion of breadcrumbs and almonds reduces the richness without detracting from the delectable whole.

350 ml • 12 fl oz • 1½ cups *each* double *or* heavy cream and whole milk

1 cinnamon stick *or* ¼ teaspoon ground cinnamon

½ teaspoon ground nutmeg and ¼ teaspoon ground mace

3 whole eggs plus 2 egg yolks

150 ml • 5 fl oz • ½ cup medium sweet sherry

75 g • 3 oz ground almonds

50 g • 2 oz sugar

200 g • 7 oz fresh wholemeal *or* wholewheat bread crumbs

25 g • 1 oz butter

240 ml • 8 fl oz • 1 cup white wine

juice of 1 lemon

sugar to taste

Put the cream and milk in a bowl or pan with the spices. Bring it to the boil either on the hob or in a microwave then allow it to infuse for 30–45 minutes. Whisk the whole eggs with the egg yolks and the sherry in a bowl. Gradually add the strained cream then carefully mix in the ground almonds, sugar and breadcrumbs.

Use half the butter to grease a pudding basin thoroughly; if you are nervous about getting the pudding to turn out, line the bowl with well greased aluminium foil. Pour in the mixture, cover it tightly and steam it for 1 hour. You can also cook it in a microwave; it should only take 5–7 minutes but consult your own microwave handbook for temperature settings.

To make the sauce melt the rest of the butter in a pan with the wine, lemon juice and sugar to taste. Allow it to cook for several minutes. Turn the pudding out onto a warmed dish and serve accompanied by the hot wine sauce.

RIBBON JELLIES
SERVES SIX

One of the attractions of a ball at the Assembly Rooms in Bath, or indeed anywhere else, was the tables laden with jellies, creams and ices to tempt the revellers. Syllabubs and whips, trifles and jellies, each more luscious than the one before, especially if they could be decorated, or striped like this 'ribbon' jelly.

35 g • scant 1½ oz powdered gelatine

3 tablespoons black treacle *or* molasses

1 tablespoon dark rum

4 teaspoons dark brown sugar

40 g • 1½ oz toasted nibbed, *or* finely chopped, almonds

750 ml • 25 fl oz • 3 cups double *or* heavy (*or* whipping) cream

1–2 tablespoons castor *or* superfine sugar

Put half the gelatine in a measuring jug mixed with the treacle, rum and 2 teaspoons of the dark brown sugar. Make this up to 750 ml • 25 fl oz • 3 cups with water. Put the jug in a pan of boiling water and heat gently till the sugar and gelatine are melted. Remove from the heat, add the almonds and pour half the mixture into the bottom of six glasses (preferably stemmed). Put them in the fridge to set. Leave the rest of the mixture out of the fridge.

Meanwhile, put the rest of the gelatine with the cream in another bowl and add sugar to taste. Heat this mixture in hot water till the gelatine is melted and set aside, out of the fridge.

When the first layer of dark jelly is absolutely set and the cream mixture is cool, carefully spoon half of the cream mixture on top of the dark jelly and return to the fridge to set. Repeat the performance with the rest of the dark and the cream mixtures, making absolutely sure that each layer is thoroughly set before adding the next one. If any of the mixtures start to set before they have been used just remelt them gently in some boiling water.

Chill until ready to serve then sprinkle the top with the remaining dark brown sugar.

A SYLLABUB

SERVES SIX

Syllabubs were popular from the mid-seventeenth century onwards and were often 'milked direct from the cow'. Horace Walpole, the great eighteenth-century wit and letter writer, took some French visitors, as a special English treat, down his garden at Strawberry Hill and had a syllabub 'milked' for them from his personal herd of cows.

The principle of a syllabub was a frothy drink of wine, sack, madeira or brandy sweetened and flavoured and mixed with milk or cream. The simplest way to create a froth of creamy milk was to milk a cow – so a cow was milked into a bowl of ready prepared wine or spirit! Of course syllabubs were also made in the kitchen by whisking the creamy milk into the wine with birch twigs or a chocolate mill (similar to the ones which can be bought today in Mexico). In the twentieth century they can still be made with birch twigs or chocolate mills although, if you are making a lot, an electric whisk will be quicker. The idea is that the syllabub should be served in a glass, the froth spooned from the top and flavoured wine drunk from below.

juice and rind of 2 lemons
300 ml • 10 fl oz • 1¼ cups sweetish white wine
or any combination of white wine, medium
sherry and brandy that appeals
approximately 1 tablespoon sugar
300 ml • 10 fl oz • 1¼ cups whipping cream
freshly grated nutmeg

Put the lemon rind into the wine and allow it to infuse for several hours then remove it. If you wish to whisk the syllabub with a birch whisk or chocolate mill (and it does achieve a slightly different effect from an electric beater) pour the wine into a tall, narrow jug or container. Add some of the sugar, the lemon juice and the cream then whisk by rubbing the whisk or mill backwards and forwards between your hands. It will take up to five minutes to achieve a really good froth. If you prefer to use a mixer, pour all the ingredients into the bowl and whisk. When it is well frothed, taste and add more sugar if it needs it. Pour the syllabub into glasses (preferably stemmed) and leave for several hours for the wine and cream to separate. When you serve it remember to tell guests what they are meant to do or they will merely think that your culinary prowess is slipping!

MRS RAFFALD'S RICH SEED CAKE

Fine white flour did not become available until the invention of roller mills in the mid-nineteenth century so Mrs Raffald's cake would have been made with a wholemeal or wholewheat flour. If you wish for a 'finer' cake substitute plain white flour for the wholemeal or use half and half.

225 g • 8 oz soft butter *or* low fat margarine
175–225 g • 6–8 oz (depending on how sweet you like your cakes) sugar
4 eggs, separated
25 g • 1 oz carraway seeds
1 level teaspoon *each* of ground nutmeg and cinnamon
225 g • 8 oz plain wholemeal *or* wholewheat flour

Beat the butter with the sugar till it is light and fluffy. Add the egg yolk with the carraway seeds and the spices and mix well. Whisk the whites till they just hold their shape and fold them into the mixture along with the flour. Make sure they are well mixed. Spoon the mixture into a well greased, loose-bottomed round or oblong cake tin. If you are concerned about getting it out, line the tin with greased greaseproof paper. Bake the cake for 1 hour in a moderate oven (180°C • 350°F • Gas Mark 4) or till a skewer comes out clean. Remove it from the tin and allow it to cool on a rack before cutting.

PEPPERMINT WATER
FROM MRS L.
MAKES 300 ML • 10 FL OZ • 2¼ CUPS

In the original of this recipe Mrs L. would have had to distill her spirit as well as flavour it; our lives are much easier. A fairly pure spirit is to be recommended but the principle could be applied to anything. According to Richard Bradley who recorded the recipe: 'This is an incomparable pleasant Dram, tasting like Ice, or Snow, in the Mouth, but creates a fine warmth in the Stomach, and yields a refreshing Flavour.'

300 ml • 10 fl oz • 2¼ cups vodka, gin *or* whatever other spirit you fancy
20 large, fresh mint leaves, chopped roughly
4 lumps of sugar

Put the spirit with the mint leaves and sugar in a well sealed bottle or jar and leave for at least 4 weeks before sampling. The spirits should be drunk as a liqueur and the mint leaves can be strained out or not as you prefer.

MRS RAFFALD'S LEMONADE WITH WINE
MAKES 1.2 LITRES • 2 PINTS • 5 CUPS

A deliciously refreshing summer drink. If you want to keep it non alcoholic merely substitute more water for the wine.

6 lemons
900 ml • 30 fl oz • 3¾ cups water
100 g • 4 oz sugar
300 ml • 10 fl oz • 1¼ cups dry white wine
strained juice of 1 large *or* 2 small oranges

Peel the lemons and put the rinds with 600 ml • 20 fl oz • 2½ cups of the water in a pan. Bring them to the boil and simmer for 5 minutes. Remove the pan from the heat, add the sugar and stir until it has melted. Add the juice of the lemons and the rest of the water and allow the mixture to cool. Strain it into a jug, add the wine and the strained orange juice and chill thoroughly before serving.

MRS RAFFALD'S GRAPES PRESERVED IN BRANDY

This is more a sweetmeat to be savoured, one by one, after dinner with a cup of coffee, but enthusiasts would, no doubt, be able to down a whole dishful.

450 g • 1 lb small white seedless grapes
100 g • 4 oz sugar
300 ml • 10 fl oz cheap brandy

Remove all stalks from the grapes and make sure none are bruised. Put them in one or two jars with equal amounts of the sugar and the brandy. Cover them with a well-fitting screw lid and leave them for 3 to 4 weeks before sampling. Serve in a small silver or crystal bowl with cocktail sticks to spear the grapes. The brandy and sugar mixture can be reused for more grapes, if it has not been drunk, although you might want to add a little extra sugar.

IMPERIAL CHINA

In a country as vast, and as old, as China it is impossible to get more than the faintest aroma of its fine and delicate cooking in a few recipes. Especially since the court cuisine of the later emperors demanded cooks with years of training and experience to achieve the paper thin shredding of ingredients, the intricate and elaborate combinations of spices and flavours for sauces and the highly decorative arrangements of the foods required for a formal banquet. In the later periods of the Mongol, Ming and Manchu dynasties (1271–1911) the imperial kitchen staff responsible for such banquets could run into thousands.

Cooking in China, as elsewhere, started with roasting meats – either on open spits or buried in underground pits previously heated with fires. By the first millennium BC (the Chou and Shang dynasties) metal cauldrons on tripods suspended over the fire were in use to brew slow cooking soups and stews. The development of this *ting* or cauldron allowed grains (mainly millet and rice) to be steamed over boiling water or the pot of soup. It also allowed for the first refinement in Chinese cookery in the separation of the different fats (pig, chicken, dog etc.) which congealed on the top of the *keng* or stew when it cooled. These different flavoured fats were to form the basis of the intricate sauces developed in later Chinese cuisine.

The most dramatic changes came during the period of the 'warring kingdoms' in the first centuries AD when the need for more sophisticated weapons led to the development of thin beaten metal; and hence the thin beaten metal of the *wok* which allows finely shredded ingredients to be cooked at high speed in hot oil. At more or less the same moment an efficient milling process was developed opening the way for noodles, pastas and breads. Interestingly, the first recorded millionaires, who 'flourished' during the early Han dynasty (third

MENU

A KENG OF DRESSED MEAT WITH
SPRING ONIONS OR SCALLIONS

EMPEROR CHIEN-LUNG'S QUICK
FRIED SHRIMPS

ROYAL CONCUBINE CHICKEN
OR
TUNG-PO PORK

TASAI MI OR SWEETER THAN
HONEY

MUTTON PASTE WITH NOODLES

QUICK FRIED SHREDDED MARROW

STEAMED RICE OR MILLET

FRESH FRUITS

CHINA TEA

century BC) when taxes were levied only on land, were either ironmongers or millers!

The subsequent history of Chinese food follows an ever greater refinement and elaboration of the techniques of speedy stir frying accompanied by the subtle development of sauces to flavour the slow cooked dishes tracing their origins back to the keng of an earlier period. By the Sung dynasty in the eleventh to thirteenth centuries, food and its relationship to the well being of both body and spirit, had assumed the central position in Chinese thought which it retains to this day.

A Chinese meal has few connections with Western traditions. One or more soups, often thin and delicate broths, form the main liquid element. Although the Chinese are quite heavy imbibers of alcohol (rice wines, a few grape wines and various spirits) they seldom drink with a meal. Tea, which was already popular in the Han dynasty (c. 220 BC–c. 200 AD) remains the most prestigious of drinks and is taken both before and after a meal but seldom with it.

Fruits (peaches, plums, cherries, melons and the venerable lychee or litchi to mention only a few) should be available on the table and eaten during and after the meal. Sweet dishes, in the guise of preserves and small honey or sugar filled pastries are eaten early in the meal or between the courses as it is thought healthier to eat sweet dishes before, not after, savoury ones.

Chicken and pork are the most ancient and popular of meats, followed by lamb, duck and wild game. Fish, ornamental carp, char, mullet and in the south-east, innumerable sea and shell fish are served along with the meats. Vegetables of the onion family date back to the Chou dynasty when spring onions or scallions were often the only flavouring in the keng. Bamboo shoots, the cabbage family, mallows, root vegetables such as yams, radishes and aubergines or eggplants, fresh and dried fungi are all to be found in the elaborate dishes of the later periods.

Salt, soya sauce and vinegar are the most basic flavourings, all in use as early as the Han dynasty. Ginger root is as ancient, joined, also during the later Han dynasty, by Indian spices such as pepper, cardoman, nutmeg, cloves, cinnamon, coriander and liquorice.

Rice or millet is an essential part of any meal, used as a bland backdrop for the foods which are eaten with it; this is why the rice should never be sauced or seasoned, only the dishes served with it. Each guest at a meal should have his own bowl of rice to which he or she will add whatever he choses from the other dishes on the table. Noodles or pasta dishes are normally served towards the end of the meal.

NB *Deepfrying.* In China what is called 'deep-frying' is not deep-frying in the Western sense. 125–250 ml · 5–10 fl oz of oil is used and the food to be fried is turned in the oil with bamboo chopsticks, a metal spoon or a spatula.

The recipes are sufficient for six people when served with other dishes.

BOILED & DOUBLE BRAISED CHICKEN★
SERVES SIX

It is not until the Sung dynasty (960–1279 AD) that we have any actual written recipes. These appeared in a collection called *Shuo Fu* and, since printing had only just been invented in China, are probably the first ever printed recipes. Among them is this very flavoursome dish of 'boiled and double braised chicken'.

1 plump chicken

vegetable oil for deep frying

3 tablespoons *each* vinegar and rice wine (if not available use a dry sherry)

salt

Put the chicken in a deep pot covered with water. Bring it to the boil and simmer it for 30 minutes or till it is nearly cooked. If you have a cleaver and are handy with it (which all Chinese cooks are) chop the chicken through the bone into bite size pieces. If you are nervous of doing this, remove the flesh from the bone in the usual way and cut into bite size pieces. Heat the oil in a deep pan – if you have a wok this would be ideal. When it is hot, submerge the chicken pieces (in a wire basket if possible) in the oil and deep fry for 3–4 minutes. Meanwhile mix the vinegar and wine in a pan, with approximately ½ teaspoon of salt and heat gently. Remove the chicken carefully from the oil, drain it for a moment or two then add it to the sauce. Turn the pieces thoroughly so they get well coated in the sauce, then return them to the basket and the hot oil. Repeat this process twice more, by which time the chicken should be well tanned, ending up with the chicken in the pan with the sauce. Increase the heat and turn the chicken pieces briskly till any excess moisture has evaporated and serve at once.

A KENG OF DRESSED MEAT★

SERVES SIX

This 'keng' or stew would have been cooked long and slowly over the open fire and probably bulked out with millet to serve as a main meal. Within the context of a Chinese meal you could use it as a soup.

450 g • 1 lb well-trimmed pork, mutton *or* lamb
2.5 cm • 1 inch piece of ginger root, peeled and sliced
1.25 litres • 2½ pints • 6 cups water
12–18 spring onions *or* scallions, depending on size, trimmed and chopped roughly
120 ml • 3 fl oz • ⅓ cup vinegar
½ teaspoon *each* of ground pepper and nutmeg
approximately 2 teaspoons salt

Cut the trimmed meat into rectangles not more than 2.5 cm • 1 inch long, lay it between two sheets of greaseproof paper and beat it with the flat of a cleaver. Put the meat, with the ginger root, in a deep pot. Add the water, bring it to the boil and simmer it for 45 minutes. Add the spring onions or scallions, the vinegar and spices, and salt to taste. Continue to cook for a further 15 minutes before serving. The keng will improve in flavour if left for at least 24 hours before it is served.

QUICK FRIED SHRIMPS *
SERVES SIX

The speedy frying of the shellfish in this recipe, delicately spiced with the ginger and soya but with an added Szechwan flash of heat from the upper reaches of the river, is typical of the cooking of the lower Yangtze river. A dish no doubt savoured by the Ching Emperor Chien-Lung when he made his famous anonymous tour of the Yangtze region in the mid-eighteenth century.

750 g • 1¼ lb shrimp *or* prawns, fresh (cooked and shelled) *or* frozen (defrosted, drained and dried) – halved if they are large
1 teaspoon salt
½ teaspoon chili *or* cayenne pepper
1½ tablespoons cornflour *or* cornstarch
1 tablespoon sesame oil
3 tablespoons vegetable oil
2–3 spring onions *or* scallions, finely chopped
15 g • ½ oz fresh ginger root, peeled and chopped fine
2 teaspoons sugar
2 tablespoons light soya sauce
3 tablespoons rice wine (if not available substitute dry sherry)

Mix the salt, cayenne, cornflour and sesame oil and toss the prawns well in this mixture. Heat the vegetable oil in a frying pan *or* wok. When it is hot, add the shrimps and stir fry them quickly for 1–2 minutes. Add the onions, ginger, sugar, soya sauce and rice wine and continue to cook over a high heat for another 30 seconds. Serve at once.

TUNG-PO PORK ★
SERVES SIX

This dish is named after the Sung dynasty poet Su Tung-Po who lived between 1036 and 1101. At one point in his career he was exiled to South China where he was forced to do all his own cooking; this dish was, reputedly, his own creation. The meat may be rather fatty for some western taste. If so remove and discard the fat once the dish is cooked; you should not discard it before cooking as the fat gives much of the flavour to the meat and sauce.

1 kg • 2½ lb belly pork

2 teaspoons salt

4½ tablespoons soya sauce

4 tablespoons rice wine (if not available, use dry sherry)

8 tablespoons good chicken *or* meat stock

3 teaspoons sugar

3–5 stalks spring onion *or* scallion, depending on size, chopped small

15 g • ½ oz fresh root ginger, shredded

Cut the meat into six equal size pieces and salt it well on both sides; set it aside for a couple of hours. Put the pork into a pot, cover it with water, bring it to the boil, skim it, simmer it for 5 minutes and drain. Mix the soya sauce, rice wine, stock and sugar well together. Place the pork, skin side down, in a heatproof bowl or the top of the double saucepan. Pour over the marinade and sprinkle the ginger and onions over the top. If you are using a bowl, cover it with greaseproof paper or foil, put it in a steamer and steam for 1½ hours. If you are using a double saucepan, cover the pan with a lid or foil and steam for 1½ hours. Remove the pork from the marinade and strain out the ginger and onion (in classic chinese cooking you use such things only to give flavour to the sauce, not to eat). Replace the pork, skin side up, with the marinade, two pieces sitting on top of the other four, and continue to steam for a further hour before serving.

ROYAL CONCUBINE DRUNKEN CHICKEN*

SERVES SIX

This dish is said to be named after Yan Kwei-fei, a favourite concubine of the Tang dynasty (618–907 AD) Emperor, Ming Huang. She was thought to have so distracted the emperor from the high affairs of state as to precipitate the great An Lu Shan rebellion. Her punishment was to be garrotted by the emperor's retreating troops!

1 plump chicken

salt

vegetable oil for deep frying

5 tablespoons soya sauce

600 ml • 1 pint • 2½ cups rice wine (if not available use dry sherry)

300 ml • 10 fl oz • 1¼ cups good chicken stock

3 teaspoons sugar

25 g • 1 oz piece of fresh root ginger, peeled and sliced

Clean the chicken and rub it thoroughly with salt, inside and out; leave to stand for 2 hours. Fill a deep pot with water, bring it to the boil and lower in the chicken. Bring it back to the boil and simmer for 7–10 minutes, depending on the size of the chicken; remove it and drain it thoroughly. Heat the oil thoroughly in a wok *or* deep fryer. Put the chicken in a wire basket, if possible, and lower it into the hot fat; deep fry it for 6–8 minutes or till it is well tanned all over. You may find that you have to do half at a time if you do not have a large enough pan. Remove the chicken and drain it once more.

Mix the soya sauce with the sugar and half each of the wine and stock. Put the bird in an oven-proof casserole or pot and pour over the marinade with the ginger slices. Cover the pot and cook it in a moderate oven (150°C • 325°F • Gas Mark 3) for 1 hour, turning it in the marinade after half an hour. Add the remaining wine and stock and cook for a further 45 minutes by which time the chicken should be tender enough to eat with chopsticks. Serve the bird straight to the table in its juices.

TASAI MI
or SWEETER THAN HONEY★

SERVES SIX

In 1772, during an inspection of the Great Wall, the Emperor Chien Lung shot three deer which were passed to the Imperial Travelling Kitchen to deal with. So delicious was the dish they devised that the emperor exclaimed: 'This is sweeter than honey!' If venison is not available, mutton or lamb make an excellent substitute.

750 g • 1½ lb venison, mutton or lamb

2 teaspoons soya sauce

2½ teaspoons cornflour or cornstarch

2 teaspoons water

1 egg yolk

vegetable oil for deep frying

25 g • 1 oz peeled root ginger

1 tablespoon sugar

1 tablespoon vinegar

2 teaspoons rice wine or dry sherry

3 teaspoons peanut oil

Cut the meat into thin strips, not more than 2.5 cm • 1 inch long and put them in a bowl. Mix the cornflour with the water, egg yolk and 1 teaspoon of the soya sauce and toss the meat in this mixture.

Chop the ginger root and squeeze its juice from it in a garlic press. Mix this juice with the remaining soya sauce, sugar, vinegar and rice wine. Heat the oil in a wok or deep fryer. Deep fry the strips of meat with their coating in two or three batches – in a wire basket, if possible – separating the pieces with chopsticks or a knife point, for 1 minute per batch. Remove them and drain them on kitchen paper towel. Heat a couple of tablespoons of vegetable oil in another wok or shallow frying pan. When it is hot add the meat with its sauce, stir them quickly together for 15 seconds, add the peanut oil, stir fry for another 15 seconds and serve.

SPICED MUTTON PASTE WITH NOODLES *or* TOASTS★

SERVES SIX

A favourite of the Manchurian emperors, the spread can be used with noodles or served as a snack on pieces of toast. Its flavour matures deliciously with keeping so try to make it at least forty-eight hours before you want to use it.

1 kg • 2 lb mutton *or* lamb, trimmed and cubed – it does not need to be a very expensive cut as it will be minced

½ teaspoon five spice powder

3 pieces dried tangerine peel

2 cm • ¾ inch liquorice root

3 pieces cardamon

1.5 litres • 2½ pints • 6 cups water

150 ml • 5 fl oz • ⅔ cup dark soya sauce

1 teaspoon salt

5 spring onions *or* scallions, roughly chopped

2 tablespoons chopped fresh root ginger

vegetable oil for deep frying

Put the mutton or lamb in a deep pot with the five-spice powder, tangerine peel, liquorice and cardamom wrapped in a cloth bag or secured in a tea infuser. Add the water and bring the mixture to the boil. Add the salt, soya sauce, onions and ginger and simmer for approximately two hours. Remove the bag of spices and discard it. Remove the meat with a slotted spoon, drain it and dry it well. Heat the oil in a wok or deep fryer and deep fry the meat pieces in hot oil for 7–8 minutes or till they are well tanned. Drain them and purée them in a pestle and mortar or a food processor. Return the purée to the stock pot and continue to cook slowly till almost all the liquid has evaporated. Store the paste in a jar in the refrigerator and serve it cold with toast or warm over lightly boiled egg noodles.

QUICK FRIED SHREDDED MARROW★

SERVES SIX

Another recipe from the *Shuo Fu* or *Encyclopedia of Sung Dynasty Miscellanies*, as far as we know, the first Chinese cook book.

1 kg • 2 lb young marrow *or* courgettes *or zucchini* topped, tailed, wiped and shredded into
thin strips

4 tablespoons yellow bean paste

1 level teaspoon salt

2 teaspoons sugar *optional*

40 g • 1½ oz fresh root ginger,
peeled and shredded finely

chopped whites of 12 spring onions
or scallions

2 leeks, very finely sliced

1 × 200 g • 7 oz tin of bamboo shoots, well
drained

4 tablespoons sesame oil

Mix the marrow or courgettes with the salt, sugar if you're using it and yellow bean paste. Then add the shredded ginger, onions, leeks and bamboo shoots and mix again. Heat the oil in a wok or wide frying pan and when it is very hot add the vegetables. Stir fry them briskly for a couple of minutes before serving.

BOILED RICE *or* MILLET

Allow 50 g • 2 oz dry white rice *or* whole millet per person – if there is too much it can easily be resteamed and used again. Do not salt your cooking water; Chinese grains should be totally bland so as not to mask the flavours of the dishes which they accompany.

Cook the rice in plenty of fast boiling water for 7–10 minutes or till it is soft without being mushy. Transfer it to the top of a steamer or a sieve over gently boiling water, cover it with a cloth, foil or lid and keep it warm till you need to use it.

Cook the millet in a couple of tablespoons of peanut or vegetable oil for a few minutes. Then add approximately 90 ml • 3 fl oz • ⅓ cup of water for every 25 g • 1 oz of millet. Bring to the boil and simmer without stirring till the millet is soft; add a little more water if it looks like drying up. As for the rice, transfer to a steamer to keep warm (or reheat) till it is needed.

COOKS, COOKERY WRITERS AND FURTHER READING

APICIUS Collection of recipes and *formulae* dating back to Imperial Rome, much copied and of uncertain authorship. There are several paperback editions now available each with translations, introductions and explanations. For example, *Cooking and Dining in Imperial Rome*, Vehling, J. D (ed.). Dover Publications 1978.

ATHENEAUS An Egyptian-Roman living in the 2nd century AD who catalogued a vast and rambling collection of information about the life style of the Ancient Greeks in the 25 volumes of his *Deipnosophistae*. It was published in an English translation by Charles Burton Gulick by Heinemann in 1927, reprinted in 1951, but copies are hard to come by.

BENGHIAT, SUZY *Middle Eastern Cookery*. An interesting and informative book on the food of the Mediterranean basin. Weidenfeld and Nicolson 1984.

BRADLEY, PROF. RICHARD Professor Bradley was appointed Cambridge's first Professor of Botany in 1724 from whence he published many books on botany as well as *The Country Housewife and Lady's Director* (1727 and 1732). Facsimile reprint by Prospect Books 1980.

CHANG, PROFESSOR K.C. ed. *Food in Chinese Culture, Anthropological and Historical Perspectives*. A fascinating series of essays, some by Professor Chang, on the development of Chinese eating habits. Yale University Press 1977.

CONTE, ANNA DEL Italian food historian and cook living in London. Author of various Italian cookery books (*Pasta Perfect* and *The Good Housekeeping Book of Italian Food*) and currently at work on an *Encyclopaedia of Italian Gastronomy*.

DARBY, WILLIAM J. GHALIOUNGUI, PAUL AND GREVETTI, LOUIS *Food: Gift of Osiris*. A very scholarly (and expensive) 2 volume work on the history of Egyptian food. Academic Press 1977.

FORME OF CURY Collection of recipes written down by Richard II of England's scribes in approximately 1399. With Tallevent's *Le Viandier*, the basis of all medieval culinary literature. Available in the Warner edition of 1791 reprinted in facsimile by Prospect Books and as *Curye on Inglysch*, edited by Constance Hieatt and Sharon Butler and published by the OUP 1985.

GLASSE, HANNAH Another of the energetic eighteenth-century lady cooks. Her *Art of Cookery Made Plain and Easy* published in 1747 is a classic of good sense and excellent recipes. Facsimile reprint by Prospect Books 1983.

HARTLEY, DOROTHY Classic book on the history of English food, *Food in England*, first published in 1954 but still available. Futura Publications 1985. Also any of her other works are worth reading.

HAROUTUNIAN, ARTO der. Several books on Middle Eastern food: *North African Cookery*, Century Publishing Company 1985; *Middle Eastern Cookery*, Century Publishing Company 1982; etc., all worth reading.

HOWE, ROBIN *Greek Cooking*. Interesting and informative book on Greek food first published in 1960 but still available in paperback. Mayflower 1972.

KETCHAM WHEATON, BARBARA *Savouring the Past*. Chatto and Windus Hogarth Press 1983. Published in the United States by The University of Pennsylvania Press.

LO, KENNETH Kenneth Lo was born in China and came to England in 1936. He has written innumerable books on Chinese food (many available in paperback), runs a successful restaurant (Memories of China) and cookery school in London and is an avid veteran tennis player.

MALLOS, TESS *Complete Middle East Cookbook*. Very comprehensive and interesting. Lansdowne International, Australia 1985.

MCKENDRY, MAXIME *Seven Hundred Years of English Cooking* first published 1973, reprinted 1983. Interesting combination of recipes and history.

MESSISBUGO, CRISTOFORO *Scalco* or steward to the Renaissance Este family at Ferrara, his *Libro Novo* was published in the late sixteenth century.

NICHOLS, LOURDES *Mexican Cookery*. Excellent book on contemporary Mexican food. First published 1984, Fontana paperback 1986.

NOTT, JOHN *The Cook's Dictionary* published in 1726. A very comprehensive compendium of eighteenth-century recipes. Facsimile reprint 1980 by Laurence Rivington.

ORTIZ, ELISABETH LAMBERT English writer, journalist and expert on Latin American cooking, married to a Mexican but living in London. Any of her books are worth reading, but especially her *Book of Latin American Cooking* first published in 1969 but available also in paperback. J. Norman: Hale 1984.

PAGE, R.I. *Life in Anglo Saxon England*, an excellent background study. Batsford 1970.

RAFFALD, MRS ELIZABETH 1733–81. Mother of 13 daughters, opened the first English catering business and domestic agency from a room over a public house in her native Manchester. Published *The Experienced English Housekeeper* in 1769. Facsimile reprint by E. & W. Books/Robert Hale in 1970 but hard to get hold of.

RODEN, CLAUDIA Claudia Roden was born and brought up in Cairo although she now lives in England. Her original *Book of Middle Eastern Food*, now expanded into *A New Book of Middle Eastern Food*, is a fascinating survey of the history and traditions of Middle Eastern cookery. Viking 1985.

SCAPPI, BARTOLOMEO Cook to several of the rich

and powerful cardinals at the sixteenth-century papal court. His *Opera* was published in 1570 and is a detailed and comprehensive record of the elegant cookery of Renaissance Italy illustrated with detailed drawings of the ideal kitchen complete with equipment.

SMITH, ELIZA Author of one of the many eighteenth-century recipe books *The Compleat Housewife* or *Accomplished Gentlewoman's Companion*. It went through many editions and was the first to be published in the USA. Facsimile reprint by Arlon House Publishing in 1983.

STEFANI, BARTOLOMEO Cook to the great Renaissance Gonzaga family and author of *L'arte de ben cucinare*, published in 1662.

TALLEVENT Cook to the fourteenth-century royal family of France and author of *Le Viandier* first published in 1490, about 100 years after his death. It was continually reprinted for the next 200 years and was the basis for much medieval cookery.

TANNAHILL, REAY *Food in History*. A very interesting study of developing food trends. Methuen 1973, Paladin paperback 1975.

VERRAL, WILLIAM Landlord of the White Hart Inn in Lewes in Sussex and author of the *Cook's Paradise*, published in 1759. Reprinted 1948 by Sylvan Press but hard to come by.

WALPOLE, HORACE 1717-97. Wit, diarist, letter writer and man about town.

WILLAN, ANNE *Great Cooks and their Recipes*. A fascinating study of thirteen of our greatest cooks from the fourteenth to the twentieth century. Elm Tree Books 1977.

WILSON, DAVID *Anglo Saxons*. Excellent background reading. Pelican 1971.

WOODFORDE, JAMES The delightful diaries of a country parson who lived between 1758 and 1802. Parson Woodforde was particularly interested in his food and the workings of his stomach! A volume of the diaries edited by John Beresford was first published in 1935 by the OUP and again in 1968, and is to be found in many libraries.

INDEX